Why Pray?

by Spiros Zodhiates, Th.D.

An Exposition of Luke 11:5-13
and Related Verses

AMG
PUBLISHERS

COVER DESIGN: FLORENCE ANDERSON
COPYRIGHT 1982 BY SPIROS ZODHIATES
PRINTED IN THE UNITED STATES OF AMERICA
ALL RIGHTS RESERVED
ISBN-0-89957-554-4
LIBRARY OF CONGRESS 82-71266

Second Printing, May, 1984

IN CANADA:
Purpose Products
81 Temperence
Aurora, Ont. L46 2RI

AMG PUBLISHERS CHATTANOOGA, TN 37422

Dedicated to
Dr. & Mrs. Demosthenes Katsarkas
(my niece Eunice and her husband)
In deep appreciation for their hard work
in making a dream become a reality
in the establishment and operation
of St. Luke's Hospital
a 220-bed medical complex in the
Biblical city of Thessalonica, Greece.

Preface

Prayer is one of the greatest puzzles to the believer.

We are admonished to pray. But does prayer involve an unconditional obligation on the part of God to give us everything we ask Him?

One of the most difficult promises the Lord Jesus gave His disciples and us is found in Luke 11:9:

> "Ask, and it shall be given you;
> Seek, and ye shall find;
> Knock, and it shall be opened unto
> you."

So, why doesn't He give us what we ask Him? Or does He act like a wise and good Father to give us only what we need and what He thinks best for us. That's what we do for our children. Yet we would be so disappointed if our children didn't ask us for those things demonstrative of their age and maturity or lack of it.

The words of the Lord Jesus found in Luke 11:9-13 cannot be separated and studied apart from the unique parable of The Three Friends found in Luke 11:5-8. And in reality the parable and the consequent teaching cannot be studied apart from the Lord's Prayer in Luke 11:1-4. I suggest that you obtain also our 356-page book, *The Lord's Prayer*. Unless you understand God's Fatherhood it is impossible for you to pray aright and to understand His response to your "cry in prayer."

In this study actually two parables are examined. The Parable of The Three Friends and then the parable found in verses 11-13: "If a son shall ask bread of any of you that is a father, [observe the emphasis on the father] will he give him a stone? Or if he ask a fish, will he for a fish give him a serpent? Or if he shall ask an egg, will he offer him a scorpion?

"If ye then, being evil, know how to give good gifts unto your children (observe again the emphasis on the children — father — children); how much more shall your heavenly Father give the Holy Spirit to them that ask Him?"

As you study this book you will understand God better as a Father and your behavior as a child of God will become more comformable to His will. Isn't any father's desire for every petition of his child to be such that he may grant it? That's when a father gives a child everything asked for. That's what the entire teaching of Jesus is all about, to so conform us to the image of our Heavenly Father that we ask what He expects us to. My prayer is that the study of this passage of Scripture, Luke 11:5-13 will be used of the Holy Spirit to bring such conformity in our lives.

Spiros Zodhiates

Chattanooga, TN

CONTENTS

1. Can a Christian Be Over-Persistent in Prayer?   11
2. What To Do When Your Pantry's Empty   17
3. Three Loaves of Bread To Feed a Needy World   21
4. Invitation to a Treasure Hunt   25
5. Finding Treasures in Unlikely Places   31
6. God's Part and Ours in Getting Answers to Prayer   37
7. "What's in a Name?"   43
8. A Missionary Parable   49
9. Reasonableness, Insistency, and Urgency in Prayer   55
10. Pussycats, Lions, and Rhinoceroses   63
11. The Fear of Being Inconvenienced   67
12. Practicing What We Preach   73
13. Self-Realization Found in Service   77
14. The Dependability of God's Promises   81
15. Is There a Conflict between Predestination and Prayer?   85
16. The Privilege of Prayer   89
17. Christ, Our Great Example in Prayer   93
18. God's Invitation and Our Response   101
19. "Ask" — Don't Demand   109
20. "Seek and Knock"   115
21. "Bread, Fish, and an Egg" — Common Things with Sacred Meanings   121
22. When Is an "Egg" Not an "Egg"?   129

23. God: The All Good and All Knowing Father, Who   137
    Will Never Deceive Us
24. The Holy Spirit — The Summation of the Best   147
    Things in Life
25. The Gift: The Holy Spirit   153
26. The Giver and the Receiver   161
   I. Index of Subjects   167
  II. Index of English Words   171
 III. Index of Greek Words   173
 IV. Index of Scripture Verses   175
  V. Illustration Index   176

1

CAN A CHRISTIAN
BE OVER-PERSISTENT
IN PRAYER?

This is a study on the so-called Parable of the Importunate Friend — of the shameless friend, I would call him. Let us first look at the passage of Scripture. It's from Luke 11:5-9:

"And he [the Lord Jesus] said unto them, Which of you shall have a friend, and shall go unto him at midnight, and say unto him, Friend, lend me three loaves; for a friend of mine in his journey is come to me, and I have nothing to set before him? And he from within shall answer and say, Trouble me not: the door is now shut, and my children are with me in bed; I cannot rise and give thee. I say unto you, Though he will not rise and give him, because he is his friend, yet because of his importunity [actually the Greek is 'shamelessness'] he will rise and give him as many as he needeth. And I say unto you, Ask, and it shall be given you; seek, and ye shall find; knock, and it shall be opened unto you."

There are so many treasures in this parable that it's going to take us a while to dig them all out. As we go along, to make our point, we shall call the three characters involved in this parable "Copper," "Silver," and "Gold," after three metallic elements, in an ascending scale of values.

The setting of this story is midnight. Two houses stand side by side; in both of them the people are wrapped in slumber. Who would dream that within a few minutes the tranquillity of both would be ruthlessly shattered? Quite unexpectedly, it seems, a benighted and way-worn traveler, whom we call "Copper," realizes that one of these houses is the home of his old friend, "Silver," and he resolves to seek shelter and refreshment under his roof.

Silver welcomes him — though with some embarrassment — for as misfortune would have it, his pantry is bare. What shall he do for this traveler who has come to his door hungry and worn out?

In his extremity, Silver decides to run next door and beg provisions from his neighbor, whom we'll call "Gold." Here you've got a traveler — Copper; a friend of the traveler — Silver; and a neighbor called Gold.

When Silver knocks at his neighbor's door, Gold is sleeping soundly and does not for some time respond to his summons; and even when he does, he only growls and grumbles and bids Silver, "Quit! Leave me alone now. My youngsters are all asleep. What do you mean by coming at this unearthly hour? You'll wake up the children." The whole house is locked up he says, and Silver must go away and come back in the morning.

But Silver persists, and at last Gold reluctantly throws back the bedclothes, tiptoes off to the cupboard, and gives Silver all the food he needs. It is, he says to himself, the quickest way of getting rid of him, and so the quickest way of getting off to sleep again.

A "How Much More" Parable

Who is this Gold? Who is this ultimate, to whom Silver, the man to whom the traveler came, has gone? Gold, in one sense, is representative of God. What do I mean by saying Gold is God? Don't shudder at the apparently blasphemous suggestion, for this one of the "how much more" parables. In other words, our Lord seeks to emphasize the faithfulness of our Heavenly Father by saying, How much more is God faithful, through His infinite riches and compassion, to supply your needs, if a mere man is able to supply the needs of another human being? How much more God?

If, the Lord says, this sleepy-headed and sour-tempered man will at last yield to the importunity of his persistent neighbor, *how much more* — and you must take your Bible and underline that — *how much more* will your Heavenly Father answer the earnest and repeated petitions of the children who are so dear to Him?

Question One: When May We Refuse to Take "No" for an Answer?

This raises two particularly interesting questions: One, under what circumstances may we refuse to take "no" for an answer to our prayers? Under what circumstances may we knock again and again at God's door? I'm sure that this has perplexed you as it has perplexed many. How many times should we pray for one and the same thing?

Question Two: Why Must We Keep on Asking?

The second question is, why does God put us under the necessity of knocking at His door a second time, or even many times? Why does He not answer our prayer at our first asking? The answers to these questions are found in the

13

parable itself. Heed them very carefully, because they constitute the answers to some of the most perplexing questions we have in regard to prayer.

First Answer to Question One

First, we continue knocking at God's door when it is a case of necessity. What was it that Silver, the man to whom the traveler came, was asking of Gold, the man to whom he went at midnight? Not cake, but only for a bare necessity — bread, the very substance of life.

Sometimes we grow angry with God because we come to Him over and over again for luxuries, and He denies us. Well, God has every right to refuse us anything that is not a necessity. Think about it. We have no right to keep asking God for something that is not necessary.

Second Answer to Question One

Then, we may continue knocking at God's door when it is a case of urgency. Silver, the man to whom the traveler came, knocked at midnight. Now, at midnight, the traveler was in desperation, not knowing what to do. His case was urgent. You may come to God, over and over again, to knock at His door when the matter is one of urgency.

Third Answer to Question One

And then, thirdly, you may continue knocking at God's door when your knocking is entirely free of selfish considerations. Silver sought bread, not for himself, but to appease the hunger of his poor friend, Copper, who, famished and exhausted, had unexpectedly thrown himself upon his hospitality. There was no selfish motive involved. How many of the things that you repeatedly come to God for are for yourself,

14

and how many are for the absolute, urgent necessities of others?

Take these three rules and you've got some of the answers to your question, "How long may I continue knocking at God's door?" You may be importunate if it concerns something that is necessary, if it is urgent, if it is for others.

There are many Christians who say, "Well, I'm God's child; therefore I deserve the very best, including the luxuries I see others enjoying." And to the shame of some preachers, they encourage their flock to pray for luxuries, as being God's will for them. I disagree with all that. We deserve only what is necessary, and we may come to God repeatedly to meet the basic necessities of others in the world in which we live. That's how I read the New Testament. If you read it differently, perhaps you are trying to justify your selfish purposes in life.

THINK IT OVER

1. Who are the three characters in this parable and what traits do you discern in them so far?
2. In what sense is the character we call "Gold" representative of God? In what sense is he not?
3. Give three reasons that justify persistence in prayer.

2

WHAT TO DO
WHEN YOUR PANTRY'S
EMPTY

Our second question was, Why does God put us under the necessity of knocking at His door a second time or even many times? I believe that sometimes He does this in order that we may realize our utter dependence upon Him. If prayer was always answered at the first asking, it would become mechanical, like the pressing of an electric button or the working of a penny in a slot machine. That's unfortunately how some people think of God. Put a coin in the slot and out comes the merchandise desired. But God is not a vending machine to be manipulated at will. God sometimes requires us to knock again and again at His door in order to cultivate in us a meek, patient, and submissive spirit; and He sometimes forces us to knock many times in order that we may suitably value the boon when at last we receive it.

We must be careful how we treat God. We can never command God to do anything. Prayer is an expression of our dependence upon God, and He asks us to knock over and over again. That is why He is likened to this man whom we have called Gold, who is hesitant at first to get up and disturb his children, and unbolt the door, in order to let his friend in. God sometimes seems hesitant, so that He can find out whether we are truly dependent upon Him. He is dependable, and we must be persistent in order to show our dependence upon Him.

Silver — The Man With the Empty Pantry

Now the question arises: If this man, Gold, is a symbolic picture of God, in certain respects, who is Silver, the man who is embarrassed by the sudden arrival of his midnight guest, and rushes off to the house of his neighbor, Gold, in order to crave food to set before Copper? Is he representative of the preacher who offers spiritual help?

You know, as a preacher, I never wake in the morning without thinking of the next message I have to give, of the next congregation to which I have undertaken to preach. I visualize that sea of unexpected faces, and as I sit before a microphone I think of all the people listening to me. That's an awesome responsibility, and a great horror clutches at my heart. It is the same horror that clutched at the heart of Silver, when on Copper's arrival he realized he had been caught with an empty pantry. It happens to us all. The traveler comes at midnight and asks us for bread and our pantry's empty. I ask myself as I think of the congregation to which I shall be speaking, "What have I to set before you?" And I realize that I have nothing of my own. As man, on whom men are dependent, I have nothing to offer. How can I satisfy anyone's spiritual needs? How can I satisfy those who listen to me? They will be like Milton's hungry sheep that look up and are not fed.

In my desperation I rush off to my Friend, to my Heavenly Father, to God, as Silver did, for something to give my listeners, who may be weary and exhausted even as the traveler was, and come to me for spiritual food. I realize I have nothing of my own to give. "O God," I cry, "think of these people who will turn expectantly to me. Thou knowest that there is nothing in me to satisfy their hunger and to meet their needs. Lend me, Lord, three loaves."

"But," says a Sunday school teacher, "Silver stands for me, too; it doesn't only stand for you, preacher. I teach a class of boys, but what do I know about boys? I'm empty-handed, I'm ignorant."

Even as this man Silver said to the traveler who came to him, "I haven't got anything for you," you look at those boys or girls in your Sunday school class and you say, "I haven't got anything of my own to give, I'm so empty. My cupboard is bare. I often feel that they live in one world, while I live in quite another. As I go to church on Sunday morning, thinking of my class, my heart fails me. What can I, a mere woman, a mere man, say to them that will help them live their young lives for God, and overcome their temptations? But when I bow my head in church, I confess to my Lord my sense of helplessness, and then there flashes into my mind some thought that, when I elaborate it in the classroom, seems to interest and help those boys of mine." Yes, Silver is a Sunday school teacher, Silver is a preacher.

"But," says a mother, "Silver stands for me, too. I am concerned about my son, my daughter. They have grown up and gone out into the world. They're doing well. I'm very proud of them and they're very fond of me; but I know that just beneath the surface their minds and hearts are filled with thoughts and impulses and emotions of which they never speak to me. The world and the flesh and the devil are doing their utmost to make them their own, and I feel so helpless, so terribly helpless. But like this man, Silver, hurrying off to his friend, I steal away to the Throne of Grace. I knock and knock, repeatedly, at God's door. As a result I think of things to say and things to do by means of which I'm able to pass the heavenly grace from God to my boy, to my girl, just as this man Silver passed the wealth of his friend's house to the table of his unexpected guest."

Perhaps, when the Lord Jesus told the story, He meant this man Silver to represent the Church, and this man Copper to represent the world. And if you belong to the Lord Jesus Christ, let me tell you that this desperately needy world is knocking at your door, asking for help. Do you put up your hands and say, "I'm helpless; I don't have anything?" Or when, like Silver, you look at your cupboard and find it empty, do you go to your Friend, your Heavenly Father, and ask, "Lord, lend me three loaves?" Silver didn't give up, and neither should we.

THINK IT OVER

1. Give two or more reasons why God requires persistency in prayer.
2. Whom do you think our Lord meant "Copper" to represent in this parable?
3. Whom do you think "Silver" represents? Check any of the following you think right:

_____The world

_____Preachers and evangelists

_____God

_____Parents

_____A street beggar

_____You and me

3

THREE LOAVES OF BREAD TO FEED A NEEDY WORLD

What Are the Three Loaves?

Symbolically, the first loaf may represent comfort for the sorrowing. How much sorrowing there is in the world today, everywhere you turn! Visit a hospital. Visit a nursing home. Visit an old people's home. Visit your neighbors. If you were to go up and down the street and knock at every door, you would find sorrow in abundance.

As you and I face sorrow in others, we realize that we've got nothing of our own to offer. Our emptiness is deeply apparent when we look at somebody in a coffin, and then turn to face the relatives around us. What can we say or do when that somebody may be a father or a mother who is leaving young children behind? Somebody who, in the prime of life, has been called of God to the region that is beyond our earthly home. Sorrow. You and I face it with the realization of how empty we are to do anything about it. That's the first loaf of bread.

The Second Loaf of Bread

And then we need to ask God to give us grace for the tempted. Yes, temptations are all around us. As we meet people, we feel utterly powerless to help them overcome their temptations. That's when we must go to God to ask Him for the loaf of grace for the tempted.

The Third Loaf of Bread

And then the third loaf is salvation for the lost. Though we witness, and preach the Gospel, we are incapable of actually bringing salvation to a lost soul.

In our desire to minister to the needs of others, you and I must go to God to knock at His door at midnight to ask for three loaves. Comfort for the sorrowing, grace for the tempted, salvation for the lost; that's what we who know Christ must minister to the world. We dare not come to them empty-handed. Come with comfort for the sorrowing, grace for the tempted, and salvation for the lost.

Pray first, "Lend me three loaves, Lord — the grace of our Lord Jesus Christ, and the love of God, and the communion of the Holy Ghost." And like Silver, leaving Gold's door, we leave God's door with a perfect banquet for poor Copper, for yonder man who is weary, and for all the hungry-hearted who come across our way.

This is the Parable of the Three Friends, actually: Copper, the weary world; Silver, the man of God (you and I); and Gold, God Himself, to whom we can go to ask for that which those who come to us need. For just as Gold and Silver are well-known to each other, God and you and I are well-known to each other. The man to whom the traveler came knew a friend who could help, and he went to him at midnight. And when the world comes to us and we find ourselves empty, unable to help, we know where to go — to God. You and I who know Jesus Christ, who are saved, know people who are in need out there and they know us, and when they reach that desperate point of need they will come to us and knock at our door.

Now while Gold and Silver are known to each other, and Silver and Copper are old acquaintances, there is one thing we must realize — that Gold and Copper have never met, that God and the weary traveler at midnight are strangers to each other. And Silver, (that's you and I who know God) is the only one of the trio to whom the other two are known. You know the sinner, you know the weary traveler who comes to you at midnight, but that weary traveler does not know your God, and God does not know that weary traveler as one of His own. We, therefore, stand in between God, who has the reserves to help, and the needy man in the world.

There lies the tragedy of the ages; the world does not know God. But that very tragedy represents Silver's sublime opportunity. Silver represents the Church, represents you and me. Let's acquaint the needy traveler with God, and let's acquaint God with the weary traveler, who will find in Him the answer to his need.

THINK IT OVER

1. What do the three loaves of bread symbolize? Do these symbols represent all that is needed by a sinful, sorrowing, lost world?
2. Who are friends of one another in this Parable?
3. Who are strangers to one another?
4. How can we help to effect a change that will make these strangers friends?

4

INVITATION TO A
TREASURE HUNT

Now, there is another aspect of this parable that I want to bring to your attention especially as it concerns the 9th verse. Look at it: "And I say unto you, Ask, and it shall be given you; seek, and ye shall find; knock, and it shall be opened unto you." Do you realize what this is? It is an invitation to a great treasure hunt to which we are called by the Lord Jesus.

There are few joys in life that can be compared with the joy of finding things. When we were children we loved the game of Hide and Seek, didn't we? No party was complete without hunting for a hidden object. We were also very fond of those games where one person goes out of the room and the others decide upon the name of a person or an object, which the individual who has been patiently waiting in the passage has to guess from certain clues that are given.

Such games as these are popular because they give us the joy of discovery. Jigsaw puzzles are very popular also, because they demand a continual search for the missing piece; and the finding of that piece gives the finder tremendous satisfaction. So we see that even in the lighter side of life the desire for seeking things and the joy of finding them reveal themselves.

"Seek," our Lord says, "and ye shall find." This is the lesson He wanted to teach us through this parable. I believe that is why God, the Creator of all and the Father of those who believe, has planned for His children a great treasure hunt. This was in His mind when He created the world. He has filled His world with treasure, but this treasure is not on the surface of life. It is well hidden, and men must search for it.

From the beginning of time man has been engaged in a great treasure hunt. He has rummaged about this old house of a world, looking for certain treasures. He has not always found the object of his search, but, nevertheless, finding something worthwhile, he has been continually astonished and surprised. He has experienced the great joy of discovery. Man has delved into the earth and found coal and iron and other metals. He has discovered silver and gold and many a gem of purest ray serene — the sapphire, the pearl, the diamond, and the ruby — and man has appreciated most the things for which he has had to struggle and search the hardest.

Take your child as an example. If you give him all the things he wants, he doesn't fully appreciate them, but if he has to work, to dig for the good things of life, he will derive greater satisfaction from them. "I bought this bike myself, out of my earnings as a paper delivery boy," gives far greater pride of accomplishment than if it had come to him effortlessly as a gift! Gold is more precious than iron, the diamond more valuable than glass.

Man has treasured the things that have been hardest to find, things that have given him the greatest joy of discovery. He has had to search for and discover, for instance, the principles that enabled him to invent and use the automobile, the steam engine, the airplane, the radio, and many other wonderful and useful devices. We have these blessings because men have obeyed the seeking instinct. There are many treasures on the surface of life, but a great deal of research and experiment have been necessary before men have learned the correct use of them.

There's Always More To Find!

The wonderful thing about this seeking activity is that man can never reach the bottom of the barrel. The world and life are made in such a way that the more we find the more we realize there is to be found. "Seek, and ye shall find."

The joy of discovery is more than just finding the object of one's search, for every discovery opens up new fields of exploration. The discovery of a new planet may lead to years of research never before possible. The discovery of the Pacific opened up vast tracts of sea and land that were to be explored by generations of sailors. Even, God the Creator has made this world in such a way that the more we discover the more we realize there is to be discovered, and we can never, never exhaust God. "Seek, and ye shall find," and yet you will never have found all that there is to find.

You remember that Curie and his wife discovered radium, but men are still hard at work seeking to discover the uses to which radium may be put, and they may never discover fully, but will continue to discover.

God the Hider, Man the Seeker

But let us lift now our eyes from the material plane to the realm of the spirit as we look at this command of our Lord, "Seek, and ye shall find." In this, God, the Hider, has prepared for man, the seeker. He hides so that we can seek and find. In the realm of things intangible and unseen, but just as real as the tangible and the seen, the treasures of God are unsearchable.

The treasures of His grace are never exhausted. In the realm of the spirit there is something that stirs within man, a deep-rooted instinct for seeking. God has hidden His treasures in the difficult and arduous ways of experience. Experience contains precious treasures that men find only as they journey faithfully along life's hazardous road. When we conquer and overcome we find a treasure of God in the conquest of a certain sin, in the overcoming of a great temptation; we find the hidden manna, which may be fresh courage, new strength to overcome another temptation that has harassed us for a long time. New strength and new joy are ours through conquest. In the midst of this difficult way of discovering new things about life, men learn to tackle it with new equipment and new determination.

The story told by a certain man can be echoed by most of us: "I wrestled," he said, "all night, in the grip of a fearful sin that was slowly dragging my soul to hell. All through the night the fearful battle raged, and I felt that my soul was lost; but with the coming of the dawn there shone a light brighter than the dawn. The Son of man was at my side and the temptation was thrust from me in His strength. I arose from my knees, strengthened in body and soul, and prepared to meet anything that might come my way."

You and I have wrestled like that man, and have found new power and new joy when we have conquered a temptation, in the power of God. The man of faith can find, if only he will seek, the promise of a glorious dawn even in the darkest night.

Treasure in the Dark

In Isaiah 45:3 there is a verse you may never have

noticed: "I will give thee," says the Lord, "the treasures of darkness." Note this. Look it up. How often those treasures have been discovered by men when the heavy clouds of grief have cast their dismal mantle upon them. Jeremiah found treasure in the darkness when he, so sensitive and highly strung, was persecuted and oppressed. He discovered for the first time that true religion involves a communion between God and the soul of the individual, and not just between Jehovah and the nation.

It is in the darkness of sorrow and trial that the finest qualities in men have been discovered. The qualities we admire most in men and women are not on the surface of life; they are hidden and are only discovered when the clouds blot out the light of the sun. We admire courage, devotion, patience, long-suffering, self-denial, and sympathy, and we only find these qualities on a cloudy day. Could there be a love that "suffereth long, and is kind" if the night were not sometimes dark about us? Oh, let God help us to seek in the night, in the darkness, and we shall find treasure.

Treasures in the Shadow of Death

"Seek, and ye shall find." That frivolous and foolish queen, Marie Antoinette, did not know the meaning of nobility and courage until she found herself in a vehicle rattling over the cobbled streets of Paris, carrying condemned persons to the guillotine. Marie Antoinette found some of the richest treasures of life in the shadow of death.

And many a faithful soul has found Christ in the valley of the shadow. I know only too well that there are men and women who have lost their faith in God in a dark valley and have found only bitterness and resentment, but I know, too, that there are faithful souls who have found the strength and sympathy and love of God, even as they have walked through

29

death's dark vale. God is in the valley of the shadow. Make no mistake about it. And if we seek in faith we shall find Him and possess the treasures of His grace. "Though I walk through the valley of the shadow of death . . . thou art with me" (Ps. 23:4). And sometimes we lose the fellowship and companionship of God if we do not walk in the darkness of the shadow of death, looking for hidden treasures.

THINK IT OVER

1. Can you think of something that you had to find out the hard way, by working at it till you solved your problem?
2. How did it make you feel when you finally discovered the answer to your problem?
3. How can our trials and testings, including darkness and death, conceal rich treasures? Name three or more qualities of character they may bring out.

5

FINDING TREASURES
IN
UNLIKELY PLACES

Most treasures are hidden in unlikely places. We can find the jewels of God even in the most unexpected and despised places. The jailor of Philippi found the treasures of the Gospel in a Roman prison at midnight, when Paul and Silas sang praises to God. If it were not for that midnight experience of Paul and Silas, the jailor would never have found the treasure of his salvation. And it is quite possible that you and I are allowed to go through the midnight valley of the shadow of death, or some imprisonment of the spirit, soul, and body, so that someone else may find the treasure of salvation.

I'll never forget, when I had to stand trial nine times before a criminal court in Greece for the sake of the Gospel of Jesus Christ. One morning an old man came into the courtroom who had walked all night with his cane from a distant village to get there. He said, "Mr. Zodhiates, I came to hear you preach in court." I knew at that time that my court experience was unpleasant, but without it, perhaps, that old man would never have had a chance to hear the Gospel. Paul and Silas sang praises to God, and so I preached the Gospel in court.

Carey, the great missionary to India, found his Savior in a cobbler's workshop at Hackleton. Mary Slessor discovered the riches of Christ in a factory in Dundee; Livingstone found them at his loom in Blantire; and John Bunyan in the streets of Bedford, while he carried on his work as an itinerant mender of household utensils, a tinker.

Where To Find God's Richest Treasure

Yes, and God's richest treasure, His only begotten Son, was found by simple shepherds, not in a gilded cradle in a palace of splendor and wealth, but in the manger of a Bethlehem stable. You and I might find that same Savior while carrying on our daily duties in the workshop, office or home. "Seek," said Jesus, "and ye shall find." If we seek in faith — like that man who wanted to help his traveler friend and went to a neighbor to find what he needed — we, too, shall find.

The Unlikeliest Place of All To Find Treasure

Now let us turn to the unlikeliest spot of all in which to find God's greatest treasure, and that is the cross of Jesus Christ, the cross of shame, the hideous gallows, Golgotha, the place of the skull. Let us look upon the object of shame and derision and suffering. What an unlikely place in which to find the treasure of the Kingdom of God! Yet there is hidden the pearl without price, the treasure rich beyond compare. Out of the vilest sin of man God made His highest revelation, the revelation of a love that suffers for the sins of men, a love that suffers to redeem.

This great treasure is not obvious at Calvary; in fact the Corinthians called it foolishness. For a man who is not guilty to die for others — "That's foolishness," they said. They couldn't see the great treasure hidden in the cross. The Jews could not see it. It became to them a great stumblingblock. We must seek for it with faith and then we shall see that God, who has broken through into history in His Son, offers pardon, healing, and salvation.

Why a Treasure Hunt?

Yes, God has planned for His children a great treasure hunt. Why is this so? Is God just amusing himself? Why did He not place all His treasures on the surface of life and thus have saved man a great deal of trouble and heartache? I believe that this treasure hunt has a vital place in the eternal purposes of God. God knew what He was doing when He concealed the richest treasures of life.

Have you ever puzzled over Proverbs 25:2, which says, "It is the glory of God to conceal a thing"? I believe that God hid His treasures because, first of all, He wanted His children to know the joy of discovery. "Seek, and ye shall find." And I don't believe that the finding would have brought such joy if it were not for the seeking. Were the treasures of God on the surface of life, man would be robbed of this great experience and life would become monotonous and dull. God, you know, has planned this treasure hunt in order that we might undergo the discipline of searching. We're not called to an easy life, but to a life where there is opposition and hardship and searching on the physical and material plane, and also in the realm of knowledge and spiritual and moral values. Because of this opposition and searching, man's personality develops. It is by overcoming obstacles and searching the depths that man finds his true self, for this world is a school of soul-making.

God Is a Hidden Treasure Also

God, Himself, is partly hidden from men, and He invites us to seek Him. "God," said Paul, "made the world and all things therein . . . that they should seek the Lord, if haply they might feel after and find him, though he be not far from everyone of us" (Acts 17:24, 27). He is to be sought in order to be found. God revealed Himself in Jesus and yet He also concealed Himself in His Son. The Lord Jesus did not go about boldly proclaiming who He was — God manifest in the flesh, the Son of God — not even to His disciples. He gave clues and left men to find out the truth for themselves. He constantly called Himself what was obvious to all, the Son of Man. He wanted men to be seekers after God.

God, then, has put us in a world where it should be impossible for us to be bored. He has hidden prizes worth finding, prizes we shall find if we seek in faith, for we have the promise of the Son of God, "Seek, and ye shall find."

God Is Also a Treasure Hunter

Let us remember that God takes part in the treasure hunt as well. God, the Hider, is also God, the Seeker. God is searching for the souls of men, and to that end He has shared our humanity. He took upon Himself the form of a servant and was made in the likeness of men.

As we look upon the cross of Christ we see what our sins have done to the heart of God, and we stand convicted of sin. We realize that there is a great barrier between man and God; yet the cross assures us that God is trying to get through from the other side, and that He will find us and will lift us up from the pit of miry clay, and set our feet upon firm ground. Through Christ, we know that we shall find the treasures that God has hidden for us; but better still, we know that God will

34

find us and will save us. "Seek, and ye shall find." We are indeed seeking and we are assured, when we do, of finding the treasure that is hidden for us.

THINK IT OVER

1. In the Divine game of "Hide and Seek," we have seen that God is both the Hider and the Seeker, while man is simply a seeker. What treasure are each seeking?
2. Why does God make us search for His treasures, rather than revealing them to us all at once?
3. In the eyes of the world, where is the unlikeliest place to find God's richest treasure?
4. In what place did God find you to lead you to that treasure?

GOD'S PART AND OURS IN GETTING ANSWERS TO PRAYER

God is using this parable to teach us something about prayer, something about our responsibility toward others and our dependence upon God. God is a Father to us. Of course, we cannot be a father as we respond to the cry of others, but we can be a friend. Because God is our Father we can come to Him with boldness, but we should be a friend to others so that when they are tired, exhausted in their midnight hour, they can have somebody to come to.

Excuses, Excuses!

Are we such a friend to others? Do they feel free to come to us for the help that they so desperately need? Observe that the time at which this traveler came was midnight. His friend could very well have offered excuses as to why he could not help him. He could have said, "Well, it's midnight; I don't have anything to give you, and I cannot go and disturb anybody at this awkward hour of the night. We'll just have to wait until tomorrow."

37

You wouldn't like God to offer excuses in the hour of your greatest need, would you? Oh, no, you want God to help you. Midnight is a most inopportune time to help anybody. Yet, with God, there is no inconvenient time. Let there be no inconvenient time for us either. Somebody is knocking at our door. Perhaps life is dependent upon our immediate help. If we delay, if we excuse ourselves by saying we are incapable of help, that person may die. Although it is midnight, an inconvenient and inopportune time, let us consider the need of others and not our own convenience.

Some people say, "Well, I'm going to serve the Lord later on. I have plenty of time. It's inconvenient for me to do anything now. But, if we wait for a convenient time to help others, we will never help anybody. God wants us to do it in spite of any inconvenience it may cause us.

Don't Abuse God's Generosity

There is yet another truth that I want to point out. Notice that it was a friend who came to a neighbor to ask help for someone who was a total stranger to the man who provided the three loaves. He didn't know the traveler and the traveler didn't know him. But there was someone in between who caused an unknown person to be helped by somebody else.

And this is what we must do. Even if the traveler is a stranger, we must help. Asking on behalf of a stranger is Christlike. God, of course, is not a stranger to us. But we can go to Him, to ask on behalf of someone who is a stranger to Him. We stand in between, so that God can help strangers and that strangers may be helped by God. Would to God that this were every Christian's role in life.

What the Lord is trying to teach us of God in this parable is that He is our Father and capable of meeting our needs.

Now observe what this traveler who came to a friend of his

38

at midnight asked for — something very little, a bit of bread which this friend didn't have. Now should the friend have given up at this point? No — that which we cannot provide, we must ask for. But observe that he went to his neighbor and asked for only what was needful, nothing more.

Do we come to God only with our needs? Or do we come to Him asking for all kinds of things? We often come with requests that are far greater than this man came to his neighbor to ask on behalf of a stranger — far greater than our actual need, in fact. We must be very careful lest we become abusive of God's generosity. When God gives us something, we are tempted to ask for more, and more, and more.

Give What You Have and God Will Multiply It

But there is something else that we must be careful of. Let's not refuse to give the little we have; God will multiply it. I remember an elderly man who was giving very little but it was truly sacrificial. And he had a younger friend who was always making fun of him.

"Such need in the world, and yet you think that with your few dollars you will make a difference! Old man, what you give is only a drop in the bucket."

But the old man with rejoicing in his face turned to his friend and said, "Yes, all that God expects of me is my drop and He will see to the filling of the bucket."

How true! All that God desires of you and me is that we be found faithful stewards of what He has given us.

I remember another story which I've used over and over. There was a missionary who spoke about the need of giving. A farmer who heard him was so enthused that he came to the missionary and said, "Sir, if I had a hundred pigs I'd give fifty of them to God."

And the missionary said, "If you had fifty, would you give

39

twenty-five?"

"Sure."

"If you had twenty, would you give ten?"

"Sure."

"If you had ten, would you give five?"

"Sure."

Then he said, "If you had two would you give one?"

And the farmer said, "Oh that's not fair! You know I've got only two pigs!"

It's so important to offer God what we have — not what we would like to have, part of which we would then give to Him. Our fidelity is measured by sharing with others what God has given us.

Now God had given this neighbor some bread, small rolls, really, three of which were sufficient for feeding one person, one meal, a small gift. Three rolls for one man's need. That is what he gave, but he gave it in the hour of great need of the other person. A selfish, unfriendly excuse for refusing the request after such persistent asking, would have shattered the courage and the hope of that traveler, and of the one who was trying to help him.

You know, God offers us promises instead of excuses. But when it comes to the execution of our duty toward others, we are fuller of excuses than of promises. If this friend could and did succeed with such a neighbor in such a case, then we can and will most assuredly succeed with our Heavenly Father when we come to ask Him for what is needed for us to show His compassion to others. We don't have to give much to show compassion and concern. We give what the other person needs, and usually we can do it easily, even as God can easily give us of His abundance.

Now, there are several other things that we can learn from this parable of our Lord. Remember, He gave it as a result of the request of the disciples, "Lord, teach us to pray." He didn't give them a set of rules but a model prayer and then this parable. These are answers that are down to earth. They are homely, coming out of life, something that might have happened to any villager that day.

God Gives His Best for Our Best

Well, one thing we learn is that God will not give us His best unless we do our best. Consider a farmer, for instance, who is praying for a good harvest. God will not do anything for him unless he himself does his part. The farmer must do the sowing, the plowing, the watering, and taking care of the field. Nor will God do anything for a student who only prays that God will help him in his examinations without preparing for them.

Therefore, if we want to help those who are around us, let us not expect God to do it all. We say God is sovereign, God can help that person to get saved. God will not do it unless we do our part in witnessing and showing compassion. God will meet our needs in such a case.

This man to whom the traveler came would have remained hungry and helpless unless his friend had gone to find someone else to help. Oh, yes, the man who had the bread finally gave it, but it took the effort of the man to whom the traveler came to go to his house and persuade him. And my friends, God stands ready to supply the need. He stands ready to answer prayer, but unless we do our part, our best, God will not do His best for us.

What impresses us most here is God's assurance that He will do something about our prayers. His promise is, "Knock, and it shall be opened unto you; seek, and ye shall find." We should pray, and God will answer.

THINK IT OVER

1. Do you offer excuses or promises of help when God sends a needy person across your way? What is your record?
2. If that person's need is greater than your resources, do you give all you can and trust God to multiply it to meet his greater need?
3. What does God expect of you before He will answer your prayer?
   a) For a job?
   b) For passing an exam?
   c) For salvation for friends and family?
   d) For success in business? etc.

7

"WHAT'S IN A NAME?"

A great deal, if that name is "Jesus." In the 14th chapter of John we find these words in verse 13 and 14. "And whatsoever ye shall ask in my name. . . ." This is the Lord Jesus Christ speaking now. Observe, the secret is "in my name." You know, there are limitations to our prayers and limitations to what God will do for us. He says whatever, no matter what, you ask "in my name." That "in my name" is as if we drew a circle around us and said, "this is what the character of the Lord Jesus Christ will permit me to ask for." We are not to ask anything amiss, but if we ask anything that agrees with what Christ stands for, then He promises "that will I do, that the Father may be glorified in the Son. If you shall ask any thing in my name, I will do it." "In my name." That defines the limitations of prayer and the limits to the promise that God gives.

Prayers God Does Not Answer

Now, Jesus is not telling us that in answer to prayer He will grant our every wish. If, we, as children, had always been given our way and the gratification of our every wish, we would never have come of age. Why do we want God to do for us what we as parents refuse to do for our children? We do not always grant our children's wishes but we do grant their needs. A wide gulf exists between what we wish and what we need, and it makes no difference what we ask God, He has promised to give us only what we need. Not that God never grants our wishes, but He has not *promised* to do so, and grants them at His good pleasure, as a loving earthly father sometimes does to his children, when he sees that what we wish is good for us.

And mark these words carefully. If prayer were a way of so tugging at God's skirts that He would give up His will for our will, if prayer were a way of getting gratification for our every wish and whim, then it would be the most deadly and dangerous thing in the world. Not only would it wreck us, but it would wreck those about us. This is the limitation of the promise of God. He says as the neighbor in the parable filled the need of the traveler, so God will fill our needs, not always our wishes.

Your Need As God Sees It

Now I want you to notice one thing here, in Luke 11:8: "He will rise and give him as many as he needeth." Sometimes we are asking God to do as we wish, instead of simply to fill our need, not as we see it but as He sees it. Sometimes we are mistaken about our own needs. Even the Apostle Paul was mistaken about his needs. You remember he thought that health and strength would be best for him. He had a thorn in the flesh, some kind of bodily ailment which he asked God to remove. But God said in effect, "No, that isn't your need, Paul; you should accept this infirmity." And though Paul

44

thought he could do the work of God better without the thorn in the flesh, God thought otherwise. God answered his prayer but did not grant his request. At first, I'm sure Paul felt disappointed, but later he realized that the handicap was a blessing.

In Hebrews 5:7, 8 we read how our Lord Jesus Christ prayed in agony of soul for the cup of the cross to pass from Him: "Who in the days of his flesh, when he had offered up prayers and supplications with strong crying and tears. . . ." Can you imagine the Lord shedding tears? And observe what He desired: "unto him that was able *to save him from death."* He asked the Father to rescue Him, to take the cup of death away from him. "And was heard in that he feared." (Better translated, "And he was heard for his Godly fear.") "Though he were a Son, yet learned he obedience by the thing which he suffered."

Now none of us thinks that suffering is best for us, but God knows better than that. I am diabetic, and have asked God to remove this thorn in the flesh, but it has pleased Him not to do so. Maybe it is needed to make me perfect, to reach my goal better through that particular form of suffering. How do I know? Sometimes we are vastly mistaken about our needs. Let God determine what they are, and let us be glad when He meets our needs instead of always granting our wishes.

We must pray in such a way as to give God the opportunity to meet our needs. And the first requisite in prayer is actually a sense of need. If we don't have a sense of need for God, we will never come to Him. If that man to whom the traveler came didn't have a sense of his own need to meet the need of the traveler, he would never have gone to his neighbor to ask for three loaves of bread.

45

We Alone Cannot Meet the Needs of Others

Now we must also realize that of ourselves we are unable to meet the need that others call upon us to meet. When this traveler came at midnight, there was no store open, of course, no market to which to go. He came unexpectedly and didn't find his friends.

How often we say, when we hear of a need, "Oh, I'm not ready to meet that need." You're not ready? Go to God to ask Him to make you ready, to meet your need and the need of others. There was no provision made to meet the need of this traveler, but that did not mean his friend should send him away empty. There seemed nothing he could do about it, but he was a resolute man. He knew that he had no right to send a man away who had enough courage to come to him at midnight.

And you and I have no right to turn away those people in the world who come to us empty and in desperation. We must go to God on their behalf. We must realize that we cannot meet the need, but that God can. This man cared deeply for his guest. He did not resign his responsibility. That's the easiest thing on earth today, but that's not Christlike. The Lord Jesus did not resign His responsibility, but He carried through to the very end.

"Well," thought the traveler's friend, "I have a neighbor who can help me." What made him think of this neighbor? Maybe he had the memory of some conversation in which this neighbor of his said, "Boy, if you ever need me, don't hesitate to call upon me."

Empty Promises Of Help

We say this so flippantly sometimes, don't we? "If you need me, call me." But when that call comes often we say,

46

"Oh, no! Why on earth did he call me at this awkward time?" Listen, call no time awkward that somebody needs you. Be ready on behalf of the desperate need of another to go to God, the One who can help. Remember, His ear and His door are always open.

It is fatally easy to think we are living the good life if we are prosperous, if our health is good, if everything is coming to us rightside up. But the days of greatest spiritual power for the Church are not those days when it is on easy street. When this man found himself up against it, with nothing to give his visitor, he thought of his neighbor as one who was willing and able to help him. Let's go to God for the things that we need to show mercy to others. This man thought he must give the neighbor to whom he went a chance to fulfill his promises — a chance to be of help.

Are you giving somebody a chance to help you? Don't be like that woman who when she became sick, complained that her pastor never came to see her. He never knew that she was sick, and finally, when he went to see her and she complained about his not coming earlier, he said, "Well, when you got sick did the doctor come to see you?"

She said, "Yes, he did."

"Well, who told him?"

"I called him," she said.

"Why didn't you call me?"

If you are in trouble give somebody a chance to help you; and give somebody else a chance to help somebody you know needs help.

THINK IT OVER

1. In your own words, define what you think is meant by

prayer "in the name of Jesus." How does it limit our requests?

2. List three things God has promised to answer prayer for. (Hint: Look at the Lord's Prayer, which precedes this parable, in Luke 11:2-5).

3. List three things God will not answer prayer for (See James 4:1-5).

8

A MISSIONARY PARABLE

This is really a missionary parable isn't it? We, Christian believers, stand in the shoes of the middle man. This is a midnight hour. There are many in the world who need the Gospel, yet so often we don't give God or others an opportunity to help them.

Notice that when this man went to his neighbor, he stated his case briefly and clearly, and then gave him time to act. He wouldn't be put off, even though the neighbor refused him at first. He waited and gave his neighbor a chance to think better of his reluctance and give him what was needed.

Delays in Answer to Prayer

Have you ever had delays in the answers to your prayers? Sometimes we understand why, and sometimes we don't, but we must wait, because we know we have to have bread, and we are sure that God will give it. This man tested his neighbor and thus acquired a new capacity to help. There are those who need you, all over the world. Be merciful to them, if you can. Go to God and ask Him to enable you to, and He will.

Now, what was the reason for the neighbor's refusal at first? "Be quiet, the children are asleep. Don't disturb me. The door is bolted." He refused because of his family.

I'm afraid many of us are just like that. We think that there should be no disturbance of our children, of our family — that they should have all the best of everything, every luxury we can give them. We know that there are starving children all over the world — in India, Guatemala, Indonesia, everywhere. And yet we say, "Oh, if I open the door to one of these children to meet his need, what's going to happen to my own children, to my own family?"

Many Christians who would have liked to serve the Lord didn't go through with it because of their family. They say, "How can I put my family through all this inconvenience, if I were to answer the call of God?" And forever after they are miserable for not having opened the door immediately and given themselves to God and His service.

Well, the Lord doesn't expect us to neglect our families, of course, but if it's a matter of the salvation and rescue of human beings, it won't hurt to have one's family inconvenienced a little.

But observe the peculiar thing about this story is that the neighbor finally gave in, and for the same reason, because of his family. He wanted to be done with the disturbance once and for all, saying, "This fellow will never give up. He will keep on knocking and wake up all the children. It is better for me to get up and find some bread and give it to him and be done with it." Well, he did it, and I hope all of us will emulate the traveler's friend. He decided not to stand on ceremony but to knock and knock until the door was opened.

Intercessory Prayer

Now the Lord gave this parable, among other things, as a series of lessons on intercessory prayer, teaching us that we should stand between God and others by requesting Him to act on behalf of their need. What is the object, first of all, of intercessory prayer? You remember, the man said to his neighbor, "A friend of mine in his journey is come to me." Who are our friends? Was this traveler a friend of his? Although this man was in need he called him a friend, but that does not necessarily mean that he was a close friend. We prefer to call friends those who don't need anything from us.

For the intercessor a friendship is expanded. It includes those who need us, not only those whom we need. Just count your friends. Are there among them people who need you, or only those whom you need? Do you call them friends because of what they can do for you, or do you also call people friends because of what you can do for them.

We don't like friends who reveal our inability to help do we? And that's exactly what this traveler did. He revealed the poverty of the man to whom he came. He found him with nothing. He and his family had eaten up all the food they had. How humiliating it must have been to turn to this traveler and say, "We haven't got anything for you." When we recognize we cannot do anything, we must turn to prayer, strong, persistent prayer.

Interceding for Others with the Right Motive

What was the object of this man's prayer? It was solely for the good of another. "I have prayed long for the conversion of my husband," said a woman, "but he's as far off from conversion as ever."

"Why do you want your husband converted?" she was asked.

"Oh," she replied, "it would be so nice. How different the house would be."

"You are forgetting," was the rebuke, "the good of your husband and the glory of God. You appear to be thinking mainly of yourself. Pray for his conversion simply for the glory of God and your husband's need of a Savior."

Are your prayers for others actually motivated in a roundabout way by what they can do for you? Intercession must have for its object not only another's good, but also purely that other's good — not our good, through his good. You know, sometimes we say, "Lord, bless so and so," simply because we know that our lives would be easier, or that we would be more affluent, if the Lord were to bless that one for whom we pray. If churches pray, for instance, for the conversion of souls so that they themselves may have the joy and fame of prosperity that would result, is it any wonder their prayers are not answered?

As we have said, the midnight guest may not have been a close friend, really. But suppose the friend asking for the loaves could have said to his neighbor, "A friend of mine and yours, Mr. So-and-So, you remember, who did you and me so much good service, has suddenly come to my house. So lend me, will you, three loaves for him, for I have nothing to set before him?" I really think that this man who finally responded after a lot of perseverance and insistence would have arisen immediately, if he knew that it was really a friend he was helping, and that giving the loaves was more or less repayment of something he had received from him.

The people for whom we intercede before God are as precious to Him as they are to us. The object then of intercessory prayer has to be purely for the good of others, not for ourselves through others.

THINK IT OVER

1. What is the object of intercessory prayer?
2. What is a wrong motive for intercessory prayer?
3. What is the right motive?
4. Are you interceding only for the needs of your family and friends, or also for the needy around the world — their salvation and desperate physical plight?
5. Are you backing up your intercession by doing all God has put it in your power to do for those for whom you pray?

9

REASONABLENESS, INSISTENCY
AND
URGENCY IN PRAYER

And then let's look at the matter of reasonableness in intercessory prayer. The man said, "Lend me three loaves." That was a reasonable request. He did not ask his neighbor to get up and kill and cook a lamb for his midnight visitor. That would have been absurd. He did not ask him to come himself and assist in entertaining him. Neither did he ask the loan of a few hundred shekels without security to help his friend on his further travels. Had he done so, certainly persistency would not have been commendable.

Are not some of our requests to God unreasonable? Are they not, sometimes, for something other than bread — that a certain day shall be fine (but what if someone else needs rain?), that we shall prosper in money matters (but how will we use our wealth?), that our friends shall have the desires of their hearts (but are these always best for them)? These and the like matters are something other than bread for the soul's hunger. We have no warrant to persist in prayer for these things, though we may mention them, of course, with every confidence that God will grant them if He sees best — But without continual asking, seeking, and knocking on our part. And there are many other things such as the removal of sickness, the deliverance from trouble, cups of sorrow, thorns in the flesh, that are quite legitimate matters of prayer, but which beyond a certain degree we are taught not to persist for in prayer. We may pray like our Lord three times that the cup may pass away, but ever with the words, "Not my will but thine be done."

Prayers for Which We Are To Take No Denial

But for bread, for the knowledge of truth, and for the practice of righteousness among men, for conviction of sin, for yearning for salvation, for the spirit of faith, for these loaves of God's giving we are taught to pray until we receive. We are to take no denial. We are to give God to understand we will not let Him go until we have received the blessing.

Now this parable shows us that the spirit of intercessory prayer should be importunate, insistent. To be importunate, however, it must be believing. The unwilling neighbor had three loaves asked for, and more. Had he been able to say, "I have no bread. I'm quite out of it. I gave the last crust to the youngest child before we turned in," I do not see that the friend could have persisted. But churlish as the neighbor was, he was not a liar. He had the bread, and he did not say he had not. The friend, too, quite believed he had it, hence his persistence.

And there is no question that God has the loaves we want for the world. He has everything the world needs. He has the gift of the Holy Spirit who supplies the reverence, the penitence, the faith, for the lack of which this world is dying. God can give them. God is not like a mainspring shut up in a watch, a mere force inside His works, bound to work only in a

56

certain way. God is the Father in Heaven, reverencing His own law, but able to give us loaves, as was the churlish neighbor. Though the neighbor had the loaves, it was indeed a great inconvenience to him to get them; but it is no inconvenience to God to give us the Holy Spirit. To do that, He has to do nothing comparable to getting out of bed or unbarring the doors. God can work miracles, but to answer our prayers there is no need of miracles. The bread, the Holy Spirit, for ourselves and others, God can give us through the ordinary laws and channels of communication.

God Has Given His Word That He'll Answer Prayer

Suppose this selfish neighbor had at some time said to his friend, "If ever you want anything, do not hesitate to ask me. If it should be at midnight, ask me. I'm really anxious to be of use to you. It will give me sincere pleasure." If he had ever said that, the friend would have had good ground to ask; but this, and much more, God has said to us. Promise upon promise, parable upon parable, He has given us, assuring us He will answer our prayer. How then can we faint in prayer? With what boldness should we approach the Throne of Heavenly Grace!

And the friend's faith was so strong that in the face of some churlishness his temper was free from all anger. It was kindly, good-humored. This selfish neighbor was not a bad-hearted, ill-natured person. Ordinarily, he was quite ready to do a kindness. He was not a cold, proud, distant neighbor. Had he been, his friend would not have gone to him. He was not, however, perfect. To be disturbed at night, to be wakened out of his first sleep, was a little too much for him. His friend called him friend, but he did not return the compliment. "Trouble me not," he abruptly answers. "Don't bother me, don't disturb me." When pressed, he put forth many objections. "I'm in bed, the door is barred, the children cannot be disturbed." But the friend was assured that beneath his grumpy manner and words there was a kind heart that would yield. Therefore, he did not get angry, he did not reply, "Well, do you call yourself a neighbor, a friend? You're an illmannered, disagreeable fellow. All right, my turn will come and I will remember this." On the contrary, the man kept his temper and pressed, shamelessly pressed, as the word means, his petition.

We all know the man who will not take "no" for an answer. The shameless beggar. Such was this man. He did not mind the trouble he gave. The door was barred? Then his friend must unbar it. The little children whom he had tucked in so nicely and were sweetly asleep would be disturbed if he got up? Well, never mind, poor little dears. They must be disturbed; his friend wanted bread and bread he should have.

Now, says Christ in effect, "If your prayers are not answered, do not become angry or bitter or unbelieving. Do not encourage hard or wrathful thoughts about God, but just go on praying. Be cheerful, hopeful that your Father God, notwithstanding His apparent neglect, will hear and give. 'Because of his importunity he will rise and give him as many as he needeth.' "

Why God Demands Importunity

We may encourage ourselves with the truth that there are good and sufficient reasons why God demands this importunity. For one thing, He is testing the sincerity of our prayers. If we really do not want what we ask, we shall soon tire of asking. Do we really attain anything worthwhile in life without perseverance? It is not by one wish or one effort that we get knowledge or art, truth or wisdom. Importunity in prayer corresponds with, is a part of, the same order as that which requires perseverance in work. The faculty of using the gift is formed by perseverance in the seeking of it. Money too easily obtained has ruined many a young man. Grace too easily obtained would ruin many a self-indulgent soul.

Importunity in prayer greatly exercises and strengthens the spiritual life. It compels us to realize God. It causes us to think of Him and His ways. It makes us look into ourselves and stir up what grace we have. Then "Ask, and it shall be given you; seek, and ye shall find; knock, and it shall be opened unto you."

But you know, that word "importunity" is an unfortunate translation. Here in Greek it is *anaideia,* which means impoliteness bordering on insolence. Because of his friend's impoliteness, the neighbor will rise and give him as many as he needs.

Is the Lord putting His stamp of approval here on impoliteness or insolence? What He is actually telling us is that sometimes, when we are too polite, we cannot accomplish the purpose for which we have set out, the purpose of altruism. Sometimes we have to be so direct as to seem impolite in order to accomplish our purposes. The Lord does not always want us to treat others with kid gloves. The urge of altruism, the desire to be of service to others, sometimes makes us *anaideis,* as the Greek word has it in Luke 11:8, impolite, in undertaking a task that we would never have undertaken for self.

The Lord says we are to ask for others. Ask for those people who lie in darkness and who will never hear the Gospel unless we sometimes annoy people a little by asking. That's what a Christian really does. He dares to be aggressive in asking for the sake of others, not for himself. The Lord is giving us a basic principle here — dare to do for others what you would consider unacceptable to do for self. But what we consider unacceptable to do for ourselves, God tells us in His Word to do on behalf of others.

The opposite, you know, is also true. Men will do for themselves what they will not do for anyone else. For instance, in the parable of the unjust judge, a woman who was desperately determined to get her rights worried the judge into letting her have her own way. Finally, she got it. Now, selfishness is one of the strongest motives in human life, and most people will do anything they can in order to satisfy their selfish interest. But, if you are a Christian, the motive of wanting to help others should be stronger than the motive to help yourself.

Beggars for Others

I don't believe for one minute that this man who came and knocked at his neighbor's door would have disturbed his neighbor for himself. But because somebody else was hungry he dared to knock and become impolite. He would have waited until the morning if it were for himself, but for another, well that's a different story. He defied conventions and buried his own pride, ignored his neighbor's comfort, refused to be put off with any excuse, and made a nuisance of himself until his friend's need was met.

Have you acted with similar urgency on behalf of others? Have you done what this man is doing? At how many doors have you knocked, or are you so polite that you prefer others in the world to go hungry and without Christ so that you can preseve your so-called politeness by not asking? May God open our hearts to understand the teaching of His Word.

Many of us preachers who believe that we should evangelize the world in our own generation, who have seen hungry children die a premature death, are real beggars, but we are not begging for ourselves, but for others. You know, that doesn't mean that we are not refined, or considerate of your obligations, but we are disturbing others so that those in need may be helped. You cannot imagine how much more we in this land possess than those in need around the world. That is what makes us do for others what we would consider unacceptably impolite to do for self.

THINK IT OVER

1. May we ask God for anything we or our friends desire? Why or why not?
2. For what prayers should we refuse to take "no" for an answer? Give an example.
3. In what way can we serve the needs of others by "impoliteness?"

10

PUSSYCATS, LIONS, AND RHINOCEROSES

This altruistic urge also supplies the thrust and drive that turn "pussycats" into lions. You should see some missionaries on the mission field who were fearful at first, but who have since become brave. I have seen timid girls working in the field on behalf of others, daring to do what strong men refused even to think of doing.

I think of that beautiful verse in I John 4:18, "Perfect love casteth out fear." What fear? In this case, fear of being misunderstood as an annoying and impolite nuisance when you come and ask. The Greek word "perfect" in this verse is *teleia* (feminine for love — *agapee*), the love that reaches its goal. That kind of love casts out the fear of being misunderstood when you stand up to ask for what is necessary in order that others may not die, either physically or spiritually.

"Perfect love casteth out fear." In other words, that love that wants to reach its purpose accomplishes what it sets out to accomplish. Those who may have shrunk from every thought of peril or privation for themselves, once the privation has become that of other people have scorned the danger and dared to the utmost. I tell you, it took some courage on behalf of this man who went and knocked at the door at midnight.

Cultivating a Rhinoceros Hide

And the next lesson we can learn from this parable is that this altruistic urge, this desire to help others, makes sensitive people as thick-skinned as a rhinoceros. You know, the friend who knocked at midnight knew he was going to be misunderstood. What would his other friends think of his going to disturb somebody at midnight on behalf of someone else? There are some people who are afraid of being thought forward or pushy if they speak up on behalf of others.

That's the whole trouble. If every Christian who knew the need were to go to other Christians and knock at their door and say, "What have you done? Do you know there are children who are dying in India — a hundred thousand a month?"

They'd be afraid of being repulsed. Oh, yes, my friend, what this parable teaches us is that we should do good, and even though we are criticized for it, we shouldn't care. Even if our motives are questioned, even if we are accused of doing it all for self-glory, we should cultivate a thick skin. If we cannot stand up to criticism when we are doing our duty to God and our fellow men, that means that we are thinking too much about ourselves. Scripture does not teach that we are to keep quiet so we can avoid the criticism of others. There is a job to be done. There are people who have never heard the Gospel — three out of every four in the world — and there are people who will only respond to the Gospel if we have compassion on their bodies as well as their souls.

Are you afraid of the criticism of others? Are you afraid of being called a "do-gooder"? That seems to be a term of contempt today. But the Word of God tells us that we ought to do good and not care what others say about us. What does it matter anyway? The essential thing is to do your duty and meet your fellow man's need.

That's all this man who went and knocked at his friend's door cared about. He didn't care whether his neighbor called him impolite, as long as he accomplished his purpose. God give you and me a thick skin in time of need. To lament our sensitiveness is to confess our self-centeredness, and the way out is the way of service. Dare to step out at an inconvenient time for you or your fellow-Christians, to arouse them to their task on behalf of others.

Am I speaking to any preachers? Preacher, are you afraid to stand up before your people to speak of the needs of the world? Are you afraid to go and tell somebody of what, by the grace of God, needs to be done? There is a need. Get up, get going, disregard criticism, get the job done. That's what the Word of God tells us we're here for.

THINK IT OVER

1. What can cast out our fear of serving God and those to whom He sends us? (See I John 4:18.)
2. What character traits will prevent our reaching out on behalf of others? List as many as you can think of, beginning with "not caring."

11

THE FEAR OF BEING
INCONVENIENCED

Quite often the altruistic urge makes people inconsiderate of other people's comfort. You remember the story in the second chapter of Mark of the four men who sought to bring a paralytic to Jesus. They couldn't get through to Him because of the crowd blocking the door.

Did these four men give up and say, "Well, we tried and we couldn't accomplish what we wanted, so let's take this man back home"? No, they went to the roof and dug a hole. The Greek text says, "And they unroofed the roof where he was." Now this caused damage to the house of Peter, where Jesus was staying. They didn't care. They had one aim, and that was to bring this man into the presence of Jesus Christ. They disregarded the comfort of the people who lived in that home, and they went so far as to damage the roof in order to help this needy man.

Well, this midnight caller disturbed his neighbor, and that neighbor could have even lodged an official complaint for disturbance of the peace.

There are people today who refuse to do what they feel is their God-given duty because they're afraid somebody will sue them, or somebody will malign them. Therefore the thing that needs to be done remains undone because of their fear of bringing discomfort to somebody.

Selfish Excuses

We like to have an excuse, don't we, for our selfishness? Selfishness produces so many excuses for not doing our duty. Some of you may have said, "Well, I feel the call of God, but it's so inconvenient to serve Him just now. I've got children to put through school, and many other obligations. How can I respond to the call of God? Come to me, God, when it is more convenient to serve You. Tax time is just around the corner. Don't ask me to send a contribution now, when Uncle Sam is going to demand so much money from me." Did you ever stop to think that, had you given it to God, you wouldn't have to give so much to Uncle Sam?

God's Call Is Not Always Convenient

"Oh, ask me to help when it is more convenient, when it will not mean a sacrifice. Don't come to me at midnight; come at a better time." Have you ever said that to God? God pity you if you have. Remember that this unselfish impulse often makes people inconsiderate of other people's comfort. It was inconvenient for the neighbor to get up. It was not very polite, it was actually insolent, of this midnight caller to come at that time. But you know, this is symbolic of God coming to you and to serve Him, not when it is convenient, but often when it is most inconvenient. If we waited for a convenient time to serve God, we would probably never serve Him. God may keep knocking at your door until you wake up and say, "What

68

does it matter, if I wake up in the middle of the night? What of it, if my children are disturbed? What of it if my family lives in a less-luxurious home?"

I believe that God is going to hold us accountable for our too great love for comfort in America, while three-fourths of the world have never heard the Gospel, and millions of children die of starvation. Half of the children of the world never have the opportunity to go to school for one single day. What Christian has the right to live in luxury when others are going hungry? If it were only comfort, that would be excusable, but I don't believe that God will tolerate luxury in the life of a believer. Someday we'll have to give an account to God for that.

When somebody comes along and says, "There is a starving child here; there's a weary traveler on life's journey who needs help over there," and you say, "I can't afford it," but you can afford to live in a luxurious home, and to drive one or more luxurious cars, God will hold you accountable for that. Who has a right to that kind of life when others are dying, are going hungry, and would respond to the Gospel if they only had someone to proclaim it to them? Your neighbor is justified in getting you out of bed, so to speak, in such a cause. They may grumble at the beginning, but what joy when they realize what the inconvenience to which they have been subjected has meant to others.

Think again of that wonderful story of the four men bringing a paralytic into the presence of Christ in the house of Peter by digging a hole in the roof. You know Peter had a wife, and he even lived with his mother-in-law. They must have just cleaned the house expecting the coming of the Lord Jesus, and can you imagine their reaction when these four friends of the paralytic began to dig a hole? All that dust, all that debris falling into the house! You know, one of the greatest things in that story is that neither Mrs. Peter, nor her mother (that is to say, Peter's mother-in-law), nor Peter himself is said to have complained about all this inconvenience. Oh, maybe at the beginning they said, "What right do these people have to go up on our roof and dig it open — for just one man? Can't Jesus Christ go out and heal him? Why do we have to have such destruction in our home?" But after they saw this paralytic saved from sins, and made whole by Jesus so that he was able to take up his bed and walk out of that place, do you think they minded that hole in their roof? I don't believe so.

And you too should rejoice that one day you were disturbed to do something about the needs of others. Why? Because the fruit of your labor will be all worthwhile, and the reward of having been inconvenienced is that a soul found Christ, or a child was saved from death. It will be worthwhile, believe me. One of these days, when you close your eyes for the last time, it is not the luxury in which you lived that will be your comfort, but what you have done for Christ. How many people you have rescued from death, spiritually and physically — that's what is going to count when you finally stand before Christ to receive the reward of your labor of love.

One of the greatest servants of Christ was Dr. Temple in England. A young clergyman who was being sent by Dr. Temple to a very difficult parish turned to him and said, "Dr. Temple, why do you send me there? Don't you know how difficult it is? It'll kill me if I go there."

You know what Dr. Temple's reply was? "Well, you and I do not mind a little thing like that, do we? If what God has set for us to accomplish will require our lives, we should be willing to give our lives."

If you had been with me when I stood before 2,000 victims of leprosy in India, and asked how many of them had

70

found Christ as their Savior, you would know what real joy is as I looked out over that sea of waving hands, in many instances mere stumps! If you can experience joy like that, you would know it is all worth while. I told them that great story of the rich man and Lazarus, and indicated that the poor beggar at his doorstep most probably was a leper. "When he died, do you know what happened?" I asked. "The Word of God says he 'was carried by the angels into heaven.'" Now let me tell you, the prospect of a reward like that is worth every sacrifice for God.

How many times I have traveled between Jerusalem and Jericho. Whenever I lead a tour I always go that way, and I think of the priest and the Levite. They had finished their priestly tasks in the temple in Jerusalem and were going to that oasis in the desert called Jericho, where they lived in comfort. But they wouldn't stop to attend to the wounds of a man who was dying. They passed him by. That's inexcusable for anybody who represents the name of God!

But the other man in the parable — the Samaritan — do you think it was convenient for him to stop? He only had two pennies, probably what he had earned that day, and his family was waiting for him. But he didn't mind being inconvenienced, as long as he could save a life. May we never look the other way, or pass by someone who needs our help, for fear of being inconvenienced.

THINK IT OVER

1. What incident in Scripture illustrates perfectly the persistence the Christian is to show to bring others to Christ?

2. What excuses do some people give for failing to serve God?
3. What should be our reaction when God calls us to serve Him at an inconvenient or inconvenient time?

12

PRACTICING WHAT WE PREACH

One thing that impresses me is that the Lord never taught anything that He was not willing to practice Himself. I pray that I may do likewise. I remember praying that way many years ago, when I was writing my expository studies on the book of James, *The Behavior of Belief.* Sometimes, after writing a chapter, I would come down to my wife who was in the kitchen, and read her what I had written, elated over what I had found in the Word of God. And she would turn to me and say, "Spiros, now go and practice it before you can preach it." I thank God for a wife like that who tells her husband what he needs to hear.

The Lord Jesus didn't have anything Himself to give, except, of course, His grace abundant. He had no bank account, no material riches. You remember, when the multitudes came to Him, He always asked others to give what they had.

Well, he asked the rich, but I don't think He ever got anything out of them. You remember what Jesus said to the rich man who came to Him: "Go and sell that thou hast, and give to the poor . . . and come and follow me" (Matthew 19:21).

And the man said, "Oh, I can't do that!" But who lost out — Jesus or the rich man? "He went away sorrowful."

But when Jesus asked the poor, they were willing to give what they had. You remember when He saw the multitudes hungry there on the hill in Galilee, He had compassion on them. Did He call for manna to descend from heaven? He could have done it; He was God. And to feed the Israelites God did indeed send down manna from heaven. But in this case, Jesus turned to a little boy who had just a small lunch, and asked him to give it. That little boy could have said, "But, Lord, I'm going to go hungry. It isn't convenient for me to give this bread and this fish — no, I can't do it." But the boy gave what he had, and the Lord fed the multitudes.

And what was the result? I'm sure this boy not only ate far more than he would have eaten if he had kept what he had, but probably went home with much more, because there were twelve basketsful left over. It's a wonderful thing, you know, for the Lord to condescend to allow you and me to give to His work — to be inconvenienced for Him.

I remember, years ago, I was speaking at the Tennessee Temple Schools in Chattanooga, Tennessee, and I must have told them of the need of the children in the world. Later, three students wrote to me and said, "We don't have anything, Brother Zodhiates. We're going through college and paying our way, but we decided each one of us is going to give blood every month, and the $5 we get, making a total of $15 for three of us, we're going to give to support a child."

No one is worthy of the name of Christ who knows a need and does not endeavor to find a way to meet that need. Whether you have what it takes or not, you can always knock at the door of someone else; and don't be afraid of inconveniencing him. May the Lord guide you do to His will.

Our Lord's Inconvenient Call To Discipleship

Our Lord, of course, lived this kind of philosophy, this kind of life, day by day. He didn't hesitate to inconvenience others. In fact, He came to them when it was most inconvenient for them to follow Him. You remember, He came to those Galileans as they were mending their nets and bade them, "Follow me." Well, they could have said, "We're busy; we're carrying on a business here, Lord. We can't leave our nets. We're repairing them to go out fishing, and when we catch enough fish and make enough money, we will follow Thee. It's inconvenient to do it now. Don't call us at this time." Yet the Lord did call them at the time that they could least afford to leave their nets.

Then there was Matthew, who was sitting at the place of customs, collecting taxes. He was a man who was high in the social strata, and yet He called to him, "Come, follow me." (Never mind this good position you have. Quit it and follow me.)

Hear the call of Christ even at a time that is inconvenient to you. You remember the teaching of our Lord about the man who wanted to follow Him but had some prior business to attend to. Jesus had said to him, "Come, follow me."

But the man said, "I've got an aged father. I'll wait until he dies, and then it will be most convenient for me to come and follow you."

And the Lord said, "Let the dead bury the dead." In other words, dispense with the conventions of farewells and come, come right away. Don't wait until all your family obligations are completely taken care of.

Putting Christ in Last Place

You know what the trouble with us Christians is? We often put the Lord in last place. First, all my comforts and those of my family. And then, what's left over, Lord, I'll give you. And the Lord doesn't get very much.

Well, the Lord was often inconsiderate. He came and woke up His disciples while they were asleep. Jesus would not have troubled these men to lift a finger for His own comfort. He never asked them to serve Him. Do we ever read of His saying, "Go and cook a meal for me. Go and prepare a bed for me to sleep on"? Never! Where hungry men were waiting upon Him — and hungry men would always be waiting for Jesus — His service was inevitably dependent upon what the other people had as well as upon His own power. He used the bread and fish in the hands of a little boy, and with them fed the multitudes. Jesus never hesitated to disturb His neighbor when souls were in need of being fed.

THINK IT OVER

1. Why does our Lord ask us to give to His work? Why doesn't He just go ahead and accomplish His purposes without us?
2. Give three instances in which our Lord inconvenienced others. Can you think of the reason He did this in each instance?

13

SELF-REALIZATION FOUND IN SERVICE

Today, self-realization is the emphasis of the hour. But self-realization, becoming something in this world, and service to others are two sides of the same coin. In other words, if you want God to recognize you in eternity, and even perhaps desire the world to remember you after you're gone, they will do so, not for what you did for yourself, but for what you did for others. Acquire the altruistic urge. Determine to do something for God and for the needs of the world — even by knocking at the most inconvenient time at other people's door.

Now observe how Luke 11:8 ends: "I say unto you [that's the Lord speaking], Though he will not rise and give him, because he is his friend, yet because of his importunity [impoliteness is the Greek word, *anaideia,* insolence, this persistence in disregarding a person's comfort and convenience] he will rise and give him as many as he needeth."

You May Ask For As Much As You Need

"As many as he needeth" — that's the point. The Lord never promises to give us all our wishes, but only to meet our needs. The neighbor didn't give his friend anything to spare, only what he needed in order to accomplish his altruistic task.

Nothing is half so important in the service of men as to have access to the resources of God. This is one of the basic teachings of this parable. You may realize what your task is, but may also feel you can't accomplish it. Remember that there is Someone you can go to — God — and He will give you, not always what you want, but what you need.

Of course, this parable does not indicate that God is asleep or unwilling to help, as the neighbor was, but that we may with profit be as bold in our claim upon His help as we are in demanding the help of men. When we know the urge of altruism, when we feel that the welfare of others depends upon us, we will storm the gates of heaven.

How many prayers do you offer on behalf of others and how many on behalf of yourself? Just do a little accounting one of these days, and find out whether you are like this importunate man. He didn't ask for himself but for another. Don't be afraid to come to God, say, "Lord, I don't have anything to offer, but You've got what I need in order that I may be of service." There should be no timidity or presumption; no question of untimeliness should hold you back. You can come to God at any time that you wish. You will never inconvenience God. His ear is always attuned to your cry.

Now carry that into the realm of the spiritual and you will find it tragic — to fail your friend when he had counted on you. Well, God will never fail you. He is dependable. But the question is, are you dependable? Am I? Are we going to fail those who are dependent upon us? Will you knock? Will you seek? Will you ask God on behalf of others? If you really love your friend, you will. The urge will be there. You will knock until it is opened unto you. You will seek until you find. You will ask until you receive. Love is the best solvent of your doubts, as it is the test of your practicality. It will drive you to keep asking God and man to come to the aid of your friend. You may worry men to the point of exasperation, but never God. And in the end, they will respond even as this man responded to the midnight caller, and they will respond gladly; for fundamentally God and men like to be pressed into service. God is there to serve those who look to Him in faith, and we are here to serve Him by serving others in His name. Remember I said at the beginning, this is one of the "How much more" parables. "How much more is God faithful to supply your needs, if a mere man is able to supply the needs of another." Believe it, act on it, "Ask, and ye shall receive."

THINK IT OVER

1. Is "doing your own thing" the highest goal in life? Why or why not?
2. How much may we ask God for? Are there any limits?
3. How may we best serve God?
4. Who's going to take care of our needs?

14

THE DEPENDABILITY OF GOD'S PROMISES

After our Lord finished that beautiful parable of the friend who knocked at his neighbor's door to ask for bread for a traveler who had come to him at midnight, He said in Luke 11:9, "And I say unto you, Ask, and it shall be given you; seek, and ye shall find; knock, and it shall be opened unto you."

The first thing that arrests my attention here is the construction of that which is translated into English "And I say unto you." In your English version verse 8 says, "I say unto you," and then in verse 9 it says, "And I say unto you," as if the expressions were exactly the same. But in the Greek text they are not. In verse 8 it says *legoo humin,* "I say unto you;" but without the Greek word *kagoo (kai,* "and," and *egoo,* "I" from which our English word "ego" comes). You see, in the Greek verbs the suffix indicates who is speaking. The suffix *oo* in *legoo* means "I say." But if *emphasis* is to be placed on who is speaking, then the word "I" *(egoo)* comes separately also: *egoo,* "I." And that's what we have in verse 9: "And I, myself, say unto you." The "I" is emphatic there, as if the Lord were saying, "I'm the only one who can make this pronouncement. I am the only source of a promise of this kind." He wants to add the weight of His authority here.

How We Know We Can Trust God's Promises

We know that it all depends on who makes a promise whether or not we can take it seriously. Don't waste your time listening to a salesman in a shabby suit and rundown heels who says, "Oh, don't worry about investing in my company. You'll be rich in no time." Ask him, then, why he himself isn't rich. If the person himself doesn't have anything, how is he going to help you?

But Luke 11:9 is no empty promise. Our Lord cannot err, He cannot lie, He's dependable. Therefore we shall do well to listen to Him. Dependability, trustworthiness, are the first qualifications to look for in the character of a person who makes a promise.

The Laws of Nature Versus Miracles, in Relationship to How God Answers Prayer

I Corinthians 1:9 tells us, "God is faithful," or better still, in the Greek text, *pisto ho Theos*, "dependable the God." We can rely on Him. The words of Christ would mean absolutely nothing if it were not for the dependability of His character. "And I, myself, say unto you." The Lord has proven His dependability by the very fact that the laws of nature which He established are dependable. Certainly the Lord does not promise here that He is going to destroy these laws by giving us whatever we desire. Oh, no! He says, "I am the One who is telling you this, and I will give you what I believe you need, even if it takes a miracle, without necessarily setting aside the laws of nature that I have created."

Christians ought not to interpret the promises of God as meaning that He will go against what He has instituted as law. For instance, if the Lord promises to supply your needs, we should take it for granted that He will do it through natural means by the application of His regular laws. The farmer who plants seed and tills the ground, expecting to reap a commensurate harvest, should recognize that it's all made possible by God. He says, "Ask, and ye shall receive."

We are to ask to receive our food, not necessarily in a miraculous way, but in a way that will continue to preserve these laws of nature so that when we put the seed into the ground we will know it's going to bring forth much more than we put in.

God can work through these laws of nature, or He can work through miracles. But He does not need to work miracles in order to answer the prayers of His people. Anybody reading these promises in Luke 11:9 might immediately think of miracles. "Ask, and it shall be given unto you." Are we to ask for manna from Heaven? No. We remember that when the Israelites arrived in the promised land, the Lord ceased sending manna from Heaven because He wanted them to till the ground and get their food by diligent labor — something they could not do in their wilderness wanderings, but were now able to do as God gave them their own land to cultivate.

Thus the promises of God are not necessarily promises for the cancelation of His ordinary laws of supply, but they are promises to supply the end, the harvest, whether it be through the application of His inexorable laws, or through the bypassing of those laws, but never through the canceling of those laws.

When a man, in order to fulfill a promise, has to disarrange all his affairs so to speak, to stop all his machinery, it proves that he is but a man, and that his wisdom and power are limited. But He is God indeed who, without reversing the engine or removing a single cog from a wheel, fulfills the desires of His people as they come up before Him. The Lord is omnipotent; He can work results tantamount to miracles without in the slightest degree suspending any of His laws.

THINK IT OVER

1. Why did our Lord lay so much stress on the personal pronoun "I" (in the Greek text) in Luke 11:9?
2. What are the character traits we should look for in anyone who makes us a promise?
3. Should we expect God to suspend His natural laws in order to answer our prayers?

15

IS THERE A CONFLICT BETWEEN PREDESTINATION AND PRAYER?

God has made everything; He knows how everything works; He knows what everybody will do. Why, then, does He tell us to pray, when He already knows what the end result will be? What difference does it make whether we ask, seek, and knock?

The Sovereignty of God's Will

There are two things that are clearly indicated throughout the Word of God, and especially by Jesus Christ in the Gospels, and we might as well accept them because they come from Him. One is God's sovereignty. He sends rain whenever He wants it to rain. He sends snow whenever He wants it to snow. Whatever He wants to do, He does, and we cannot hinder Him or influence Him in the doing of it. He is sovereign. We can't change that.

Prayer as an Indication of Man's Free Will

But the fact also remains that He wants us to pray, and

that is just as much a part of His sovereignty as everything else. He says, "Pray, ask, seek, knock." The fact that He wants us to pray is a recognition of the sovereign freedom of our will. He has given us freedom of will to come to Him, the omnipotent, all-sovereign God, as a Father and talk to Him about our needs.

If God entered a heart against its will, He would be violating the freedom of will with which He created us. Only when our will voluntarily comes into harmony with His will can we ask and expect to receive.

Jesus Christ Is God Himself — the Creator and Sustainer of All

Now, there is something we must understand about the Lord's prefacing the words, "Ask, seek, knock" with the declaration, "And I, myself, say unto you," and that is He has the authority to say so. He is the Creator, and "in Him dwelleth all the fulness of the Godhead bodily" (Col. 2:9). Here He is declaring that He is God Himself. He is the Creator, and the Sustainer, also, of all things. As the Sustainer of all things He is able to hear us and to do what we ask, if it is in accordance with His eternal will — or even to give us something better than what we, in our limited wisdom, ask for. John 1:3 says, "By him were all things made, and there isn't a thing that was made that wasn't made by him."

Colossians 1:17 is a mind-boggling verse, which I'll translate directly from the Greek: "And he it is who is before all things, and all things in him consist." In other words, in Him everything holds together. He is the cohesive force of everything.

86

How Does God Deal with the Various and Often Contradictory Prayers of His Children?

Have you ever thought what happens when you ask something from God and then another child of God asks exactly the opposite? Take a farmer who needs rain and another believer who needs sunshine. Now since God cannot please both, what will He do? In His eternal wisdom and providence, He will answer in a way that will best further His plans. If the believer needs the sunshine more than the farmer needs the rain, then God may bring sunshine. Otherwise, He might bring rain — unless, of course, in His larger view of the needs of all, or His plans for all, He sends what is best for all. Our prayers are often so competing that when the Lord looks from above He must decide what is best from His own point of view. Unlike a human parent, He is not perplexed as to whom to please. Have you ever had this happen: one child in your family wants to do one thing and another child wants to do the opposite, and you as a parent don't know what to do? I sometimes think it is not easy for God to be God. He created, He sustains everything, and I'm glad that He sees all of humanity from above and answers accordingly.

THINK IT OVER

1. Although God is sovereign, what "sovereign" gift has He given to man?
2. Why does God refrain from entering a man's heart and saving Him against his will?
3. Why should we pray, if God already knows our needs and has determined the answer?

4. Have you ever stopped to consider whether what you are praying for is in conflict with what someone else is praying for? What would you expect God to do in such a case?

16

THE PRIVILEGE OF PRAYER

"I say unto you," declared Jesus. Very interestingly, the Greek word for "say" here is *legoo*. There are two Greek words for "say": *legoo*, which is akin to *Logos*, meaning "word or intelligence," and *laleoo*, which refers to speaking without reference to thought content. *Legoo* means "I speak to you with intelligence." In other words, "I know what I am saying, and I, myself, intelligently say unto you, Ask, seek, knock." And as we look at Him questioningly, our Lord might say, "Oh, I know you are wondering about the doctrine of predestination. Of course I know all that's going to happen, but nevertheless I am intelligent enough to tell you that it is your responsibility to ask, to seek, and to knock."

Jesus knew what He was talking about. These are not the words of a lunatic. Take them as from God Himself. Nobody else ever said words like these. Nobody else ever made promises such as these. Who else could promise that if a man asks he will be heard, if he seeks he will find, if he knocks it will be opened unto him? These are unique promises of God, the

Creator and Preserver of all things. Therefore, when He says that He is going to give us something, He is going to do it.

The Limitations of What We May Ask in Prayer

But that doesn't mean we can claim from Him anything we want. If what we ask is not something that will fit into His whole plan for the universe, He is not going to grant it, because it would do more harm than good. We can't expect a God who is so orderly in creating the universe to allow us to have something that would spoil His whole plan.

But someone may ask, "Doesn't Luke 11:9 give us the freedom to ask for anything?" Not really, for this is not an unqualified promise, in the light of the whole context of what the Word of God says about prayer. The Lord has already instituted the laws of His Kingdom and we are not to ask for anything that will tend to cancel those laws or to make them ineffective. There is a qualifying statement in John 14:13 and 14 that tells us the limitations of our asking: "And whatsoever ye shall ask in my name." The verse doesn't stop at "whatsoever ye shall ask," but goes on to stipulate that it must be "in my name."

Prayer "in Jesus' Name"

What does "in my name" mean? Is it merely a phrase we tack on to the end of our prayers: "In Jesus' name, Amen"? Jesus meant, "Within my character and its purposes. I stand for something. I stand for the laws of the Kingdom. I stand for the laws of nature that I have made, and no one can go ahead at any whim of his imagination to ask for the cancelation of those things — I will not stand for it." Therefore the things we ask for must be in accordance with the character and purposes of Jesus Christ. "In my name, that will I do." And observe another limitation in verse 13: "that the Father may be glorified in the Son." In other words, if we ask for anything that will detract from the glory of God the Father as exemplified in God the Son, our petition will not be granted. Christ knows the laws of His own Kingdom and He's not giving us liberty here to cancel His plan. That's not prayer.

Why Pray If God Has Already Determined What Will Happen?

Hasn't God already determined everything, however? Yes, He has. If so, then how can prayer produce results? After all, His decrees are immutable.

It is true that God has foreknown and predestinated everything that happens in Heaven above and in earth beneath. Why pray then? But that's like asking, if God has predestined the air, why should we breathe? The answer is, because He has ordained it so. Yes, it could have been possible that we didn't need to breathe to live, but God who has put the oxygen here in the exact amount needed to sustain life has also ordained that we should breathe; and He who has set His plans ahead of time has also told us that we should ask and pray. It's all there waiting for us to appropriate it, but He says, ask for it. Prayer simply releases what God wants to give us.

He has also predestined His people's prayers. When we pray we produce links in the chain of ordained facts. It gives us a sense of bringing to pass that which God in eternity predetermined. That's a tremendous thing to contemplate — that when we pray God does something. It proves that we are in tune with God, and what we have asked has been in such agreement with God's purpose that it has been accomplished and we are co-workers with God. The privilege of prayer is tremendous. What joy to know that we have adjusted our will with the plan of God. Destiny decrees that we should pray; therefore we pray. Destiny decrees that we shall be answered, and the answer comes. The Lord Jesus says the decrees of God need not trouble us. They are His business. He has also determined that our business is to pray.

There is nothing inconsistent with our prayers being heard and God's eternal and immutable decrees. He who bids us pray has been with the Father from the beginning. "The same was in the beginning with God," and He knows what the purposes of the Father are and what the heart of God is. Therefore, He is in a position to know that in our asking there is no conflict. He stands between God's eternal purposes and our temporal desires. He is the bridge. That's why, before saying "Ask, and it shall be given unto you," He says, "And I, myself, intelligently say unto you."

THINK IT OVER

1. What is the significance of the Lord's prefacing His command to pray with the words, "And I, myself, *intelligently* say unto you"?
2. Would an "intelligent" Deity tell us to pray, if this was a conflict between His predestination and our free will?
3. What are the limitations to prayer that reconcile these two factors?
4. What is the great privilege that praying in God's will confers on us?

17

CHRIST OUR GREAT EXAMPLE IN PRAYER

One thing the Lord Jesus Christ wanted to make clear is that He does not wish us to feel unworthy in coming to God. Sometimes we feel so insignificant that we wonder if God really considers us worth His attention.

Would you walk uninvited into the President's office to ask him a favor? You'd feel so small in comparison to his greatness. Yet though God is the Omnipotent Creator and Sustainer of the universe, He gives us the liberty to come to Him with boldness through the Lord Jesus. We are so little, He is so great; we are so sinful and He is so holy.

Jesus Our Intermediary in Prayer

But the Lord Jesus Christ says, "I, myself, intelligently say unto you, ask, seek, knock. I know what I'm talking about, because I have become the bridge between the great God and the little man." Just as somebody has to act as the intermediary between you and the great office of the President, so the Lord Jesus Christ says, "I am the Intermediary between you and the Father. You can come to Him through me. You can ask, you can seek, you can knock, and be assured of an audience because you come through me, for I am the God-man. I am the One who, with one hand holds the Father and with the other hand holds man."

Jesus Christ knows both the greatness of God and the weakness of man, for He, who was God, became man without ceasing to be God. That is why He can say, "And I, myself, intelligently, responsibly say unto you, Ask, seek, knock." He knows from experience how ready the Father is to hear us, because He Himself prayed to the Father.

Jesus Our Example in Prayer

It would be excellent if, in our study of prayer, we were to follow the example of Jesus Christ. For instance, we find Him in Gethsemane praying. Praying? He was God and yet He prayed. But He was also human, and in His humanity He set an example for us. For instance, in Luke 22:42 we read of His saying, "Father, if thou be willing, remove this cup from me: nevertheless not my will, but thine, be done." As a human being, He wanted, if possible, to avoid the death of the cross. But He is submitting His will to the will of God.

Recently I heard a broadcast on which a woman said, "I know it is God's will for you to be healed." Let me tell you that she doesn't know anything of the sort. Only God knows whether it is His will for anyone to receive a certain blessing, whether it be healing or anything else. He is a sovereign God. If the Lord Jesus Christ submitted His will to the will of the Father, it is surely necessary for us to do likewise. Let us follow His example.

I have been deeply impressed by what Hebrews 5:7 and 8 tells us about Jesus and prayer: "Who in the days of his flesh, when he had offered up prayers and supplications with strong crying and tears . . . ." Can you imagine the Lord Jesus Christ, in whom all the fullness of the Godhead dwelt, praying with "strong crying and tears"? He cried "unto him that was able to save him from death, and was heard in that he feared; though he were a Son, yet learned he obedience by the things [not which he received, but] which he suffered."

On the cross our Lord prayed, and He said, "It is finished." He had wanted to avoid His crucifixion as a human being, but the Divine element in Him overcame. His answer was to accomplish His task and not to receive what He wanted as man.

We know our human nature more than our divine, but God wants us to accomplish His divine purpose for our lives instead of receiving what we think is best for us as human beings. Christ speaks from His own experience when He says, "And I say unto you." Follow His example. Come to the Father, but leave it up to the Father to answer as He thinks best. Go ahead and ask, but don't demand. Ask, and He will give you what is best for you.

The Lord had a reason for telling us to pray, and in fact there is more reason for us to pray today than there was in the days of His flesh. When He said these words, "And I, myself, intelligently say unto you, Ask, seek, knock," He had not yet gone through the experience of death and resurrection. His disciples did not really understand or believe that He was one day going to rise from the dead. But now, the great victory of the resurrection is history, and if our Lord said with authority before His resurrection that we could pray and our Heavenly Father would listen to us, how much more can we believe Him today, now that He has proven His Deity by His resurrection and ascension to Heaven?

Prayer a Value in Itself Apart from Getting What We Ask For

There is a value in prayer altogether apart from the answers that God gives us, which justifies prayer. When we pray, we tend to think mainly of the things we hope to receive instead of the relationship between God and ourselves. The fact that we are permitted to pray, to ask, to seek, to knock at the door of God is a blessing in itself.

A thinker once said, "I have conquered all my doubts, not with my books but on my knees. Prayer would be enough by itself, even if we did not get a single thing for which we prayed. There is something in the reflex attitude and influence and effect of prayer which makes prayer a blessing in itself. Ask, and the very asking is a grace. Seek, and before the answer comes you have found something worth finding. Knock, and that very knock is a blessing in itself."

We can rest assured that, if we pray much, we are blessed much, irrespective of the things we receive. Little prayer, little blessing. No prayer, no blessing. We'll be surprised what prayer will do just by itself in our life, irrespective of things that we ask for or receive.

"Ask, seek, knock." That means pray. Pray and the very fact that we are permitted to pray has a blessing in it. "And I, myself, intelligently declare unto you. . . ." In other words, the Lord here tells us that there is something in prayer which He knows is going to do us good, not necessarily because of the answers we will receive, but because there is an inherent value in prayer.

Prayer is one of the most misunderstood privileges of the Christian. He comes to God with very foolish requests sometimes. He asks for things that are contrary to the laws that God has instituted, and expects God to break them on his behalf. Prayer must be based on a knowledge of God's will as revealed in His Word. And His will is not to grant us exemption from every adverse circumstance in life, but to produce Christlikeness of character in us.

Prayer Leads Us to Understand How to Place Proper Limitations on Our Requests

Prayer imposes an unconscious check on life. It makes us wise in the ways of God. As I was reading the story of the temptation of our Lord when He was led by the Spirit into the wilderness, I was shocked into awareness (for the first time, I'm afraid) that Satan was asking Him actually to do something that was contrary to His physical laws. For instance, he asked the Lord to turn stones into bread. Why? Just to show His power. The Lord would not do this for Himself, and He is not going to do it for us. If we want bread, we must cultivate the land and grow wheat which makes bread, or earn the money to buy it.

Then, after taking him to the pinnacle of the temple, Satan said, "Cast yourself down and the angels will sustain you, will hold you up." Here he was asking Him to go contrary to the law of gravity which the Lord Himself had ordained. Again the Lord refused. He could have done it, but He wouldn't.

This is a lesson we should take to heart. When we pray, we should not ask God to do anything that would be contrary to the laws and the promises that He has made. There is a word in Greek that is appropriate here. It is *soophrosunee*. Sometimes it is translated "moderation," sometimes it is translated "sobriety." Paul, in speaking to Festus in Acts 26:25 said, "I am not mad ... but speak forth words of truth and soberness [*soophrosunee*]." This is something we must learn to exercise in prayer. It means placing voluntary limitations on our freedom: to exercise our mind, and put around our prayers a circle of containment as to what we should pray for and what we should not pray for. Let's not tempt God in our prayers.

The Apostle Paul says in Romans 12:3 something very significant in this regard: "For I say, through the grace given unto me, to every man that is among you, *not to think of himself more highly than he ought to think.*" In Greek that last expression is *phronein eis to soophronein,* which means "he must think in such a way as to prescribe limitations to his freedom" — to think prudently.

Think — Then Pray

A man who prays must think. Should we ask God for something as contrary to His natural laws as to turn stone into bread? Is it right to ask God to perform a miracle? Of course, God is able to perform a miracle, and when Satan tempted the Lord Jesus to do this particular act, he knew full well that the Lord could do it. But it was a wrong thing to ask Him and it's a wrong thing for us to ask God to do something contrary to His laws or promises. It is far better to ask Him to send rain on the land to produce wheat from which we can make bread, or to enable us to earn the money to buy it. God can also move upon the heart of someone else to come to our aid — and all this is in accordance with His usual way of answering prayer. "To think soberly," *soophronein,* "to think circum-spectly," about prayer is to prescribe the limitations of our asking, as a result of the sound mind that the Lord has given us — "according as God has dealt to every man the measure of faith."

THINK IT OVER

1. When you look at the starry heavens do you ever wonder if God takes note of you?
2. How does Luke 11:9 encourage us to believe God does listen when we speak to Him?
3. What two functions does Jesus Christ perform in regard to our prayer life?
4. What other purposes does prayer serve than the receiving of answers to our petitions?

18

GOD'S INVITATION AND OUR RESPONSE

If you want to find how sinful you are, ask yourself how much or how little you pray. Sinfulness is directly proportionate to prayerlessness. Holiness, on the other hand, is directly proportionate to prayerfulness. If your tendency is to pray less and less, your tendency is to sin more and more.

Prayer a Blessing in Itself

There is value in the very fact of praying. If anyone abandons prayer, he abandons one of the highest forces that mold and benefit human character. You could not go into the presence of God without receiving a blessing, even if God never answered your particular petitions. Prayer contains its own grace and blessing. You remember, when Moses came down from the mountain, how his face shone because he had been with God. That's what prayer does: it makes your life shine. You do not pray simply to get certain things, but to commune with God, to be in His presence.

The Lord Jesus Christ said, "Ask, seek, knock, pray"

because He Himself prayed. You remember how often we read in the Scriptures that He left His disciples and went into the wilderness in order to pray. His was a life of prayer. The best man who ever lived felt the necessity of prayer and the best men in the world are those who pray. How much more should we pray if Jesus, the Omnipotent, the Holy One, prayed.

The Example of the Virgin Mary

Or consider His mother, the Virgin Mary. Some people say, "I don't believe in this business of being 'born again'; I'm good enough as I am." Well, if the mother of Jesus, the best woman in the world, felt the need of a Savior, then there isn't anyone so good that he or she doesn't need a Savior also. Notice what she said in the Magnificat, her song of praise: "My soul doth magnify the Lord, and my spirit hath rejoiced in God my Saviour" (Luke 1:46). If she needed a Savior, certainly everybody needs a Savior. If she needed to pray, certainly everybody needs to pray.

Prayer a Common Need of All

As far as we know, the Lord Jesus never used any ecstatic language in prayer. There is no record in Scripture that would warrant that assumption. We have so many misconceptions of prayer. Prayer is not ecstasy, *per se;* prayer is the deepest communion of our hearts with the heart of God. Jesus told us to pray because He knew we needed this communion with the Father. He knew our temporal needs were different, but this is a common need of all — that we should pray.

God's Common Mercies — Free to All

Though the Lord says in Luke 11:9, "And I, myself,

intelligently declare to you that you must pray, ask, seek, knock," we must realize that there are things God gives automatically whether we pray or not. These we call the common graces of God. We don't have to pray each morning for sufficient oxygen in the air to sustain our life. We don't have to pray that the Lord will continue to keep the law of gravity in effect, so that we may not fall off the earth. These are common mercies, and God gives them to those who pray and to those who do not pray.

The Special Graces of God Reserved for Those Who Ask

But God wants everybody to communicate with Him for special graces. What are these graces? Salvation, for one. In order for us to receive salvation from God, the forgiveness of our sin, it is necessary for us to ask for and seek that salvation. The Lord is not going to give it to us automatically.

Luke 11:9 a Conditional Promise

We must also realize that God imposes on Himself certain limitations as far as the granting of the things that we ask Him. In Luke 11:9 we have not merely a promise but a declaration of the condition of our receiving any good gift from God. God has limited His mercy. He is going to give it only to those who ask, only to those who seek, only to those who knock at His door. He has a treasure house full of grace, but we must go up to its doors and knock or they will not be opened. There is the River of Life, which is open to all, but we may die from thirst on its banks unless we kneel down and drink. The mercy of God is abundant and sufficient, but we must not only desire it but ask for it. Ask, says Christ, and then you will receive. No special grace of God will be granted unless it is sought.

"Ye have not," the Apostle James says, "because ye ask not" (James 4:2) — not because you don't need it, but because you don't ask. And the unfortunate thing is that the people who need the grace of God the most are those who seek it the least.

God Takes the Initiative in Prayer

Even the very asking of the grace of God is part of His grace, for the initiative, the first move, as far as communicating with Him in prayer, is His. It originates from God's side. He told us to pray. If we receive an invitation from the White House to go and visit the President, our knock at the door will gain us admission; but if we go on our own without having been invited, nothing will come of it. Remember, that it was the Lord Himself who invited us to ask, to seek, and to knock.

Arrogance Versus Humility in Prayer

Don't be too proud to respond to His invitation. It comes from an Almighty God, so feel free to go, ask, seek — but remember to behave yourself. Prayer is not forcing our way into God's presence. We are there praying because He has invited us. But although He has given us the boldness to pray, we must not try to go to Him as an equal, but as a loving and humble subject. If the President of the United States invited us to visit him, and we tried to assume the prerogatives of the Presidency ourselves, he'd soon put us out. Yet, this is how some of us act toward God. He has told us to ask, but our asking often demonstrates an attitude of irresponsibility on our part. We ask Him to overrule His natural laws, to act as our servant who must accede to our command. We must never play God when we pray. We must never feel we go into His presence determined to wring an answer from a reluctant

104

God. Remember, we are there at His invitation in the first place.

In our Lord's parable about the man who came and knocked at the door of his neighbor at midnight for the sake of a needy friend, you remember that the neighbor grumbled and wouldn't get up immediately. Jesus told this, not to demonstrate how God responds, but to contrast God's behavior with that of the unwilling neighbor. God issues the invitation and His ear is ever attuned to listen to our voice the moment we pray. But remember that when we pray, we are responding to His invitation. We must never dictate to God when we pray, but be submissive to His authority and will.

In the 11th Chapter of Luke, after Jesus gave the disciples the Lord's Prayer, He followed it up with the Parable of the Importunate Friend, to illustrate how we need to go to God, for we have nothing to offer the world unless we first receive something from Him. Prayer is a response to God's invitation. Ask, seek, knock. But how slow we are to respond to that invitation! I wonder how fast we would answer the President if we were to receive an invitation from him in our mailbox? Would we allow a week, a month, a year to elapse before we responded to that invitation? If we took our own good time in answering, maybe the invitation would be canceled. God has taken the initiative for the sinner and for the believer. To the sinner He says, "Come unto me, all ye that labour and are heavy laden, and I will give you rest" (Matt. 11:28). Why don't more people respond to that invitation? We have strange ways in which we treat such an invitation from the Omnipotent One.

Don't Give Up!

And how quick we are to give up! This parable of the midnight caller is a parable of perseverance. The traveler's

105

friend insisted that his neighbor get up and give him the bread that he needed for his friend. But we pray once or twice, or maybe longer, and then give up. If you were to read Luke 11:9 in Greek, it is: *aiteite, zeeteite, krouete,* "Ask, seek, knock." That's all Greek to you, isn't it? But all the verbs are in the present tense, indicating continuity. *Keep on* asking. *Keep on* seeking. *Keep on* knocking. Matthew 11:12 tells us, "the kingdom of heaven suffereth violence, and the violent take it by force." In other words, we must exercise perseverance if we are to have power with God. First we should respond to God's initiative immediately, and then not give up in our response to His invitation. We should continually come to the Lord in prayer. Not, of course, that we are going to insist on having our own way, but we are going to obey Him whether we have our own way or not; we are going to keep on asking, seeking, and knocking.

God's Response to Our Response

And then, we have something else. First, we considered the initiative of God in inviting us to ask, to seek, and to knock. Secondly, we considered our response to that initiative. And thirdly, we must consider God's response to our response. "Ask, and ye shall receive; seek, and ye shall find; knock, and it shall be opened unto you." Here we have an ascending scale. It's easier to ask than to seek, and it's easier to seek than to knock. God asks for an ascending scale of effort on our part. And His response is absolutely sure. What does our Lord say? "Ask, and it shall be given unto you; seek, and ye shall find; knock, and it shall be opened unto you." In these words we have His assurance that there will be a response to our response. God will not fail us. He will give us what we need, as He in His superior wisdom sees it.

In Luke 11:8, in speaking of the man who was awakened

106

out of sleep because of the need of his friend, Jesus said, "He will rise and give him *as many as he needeth.*" When we go to God in response to His invitation and ask for something, that does not always mean that God is going to give us exactly what we ask for, or that He will do exactly what we ask Him to do. He will give us what we need, which may be different from what we asked. He knows what we need better than we do. He will not deceive us. He will not give us a stone instead of bread, but He may give us the means of earning our living so we can have bread, and even cake occasionally! We wouldn't mind that, would we? But it's His decision, not ours. We must determine in simple faith that our prayers will never go unanswered.

THINK IT OVER

1. Name several mercies God bestows on the saved and the unsaved alike — without being asked.
2. What fundamental gift of God is bestowed only on those who ask?
3. What is the significance of the verbs "ask, seek, knock," being in the present (and continuous) tense in Greek?
4. Is your prayer life a "now-and-then" affair, or a regular and duly proportionate part of your daily life?

19

"ASK" — DON'T DEMAND

Notice that the Lord did not tell us what to ask for in Luke 11:9. He simply says, "Ask," but He didn't say what for. He says "Seek," but He didn't say for what. He says, "Knock," but He didn't say at what door or looking for what. However, the Lord's Prayer gives us the priorities of prayer: first, God's glory and Kingdom and will; second, our daily bread (our material needs); third, deliverance from temptation; and lastly forgiveness for our sins and a forgiving spirit toward others.

Open When God Knocks, and He Will Open When You Knock

Admit God into your life and Omnipotence is on your side. Refuse Him admission and you are left to starve spiritually on your own resources. God respects your freedom and stays without, knocking at your door to gain entrance; and when you knock at His door, He will surely open and bid you come in and sup with Him. But the food is not yours, it is

His. He will select what He knows is right for you. The best is reserved for those who respond to His initiative and leave the choosing of what is needed to Him.

Come As a Beggar to a King

In Greek the word "ask" is *aiteite,* and that's the word from which another Greek word is derived, *epaitees,* which means "beggar." *Aiteoo:* ask as if you were a beggar, an inferior coming to a superior, to plead for something that you could not do for yourself. There is another Greek word in the New Testament, *erootaoo,* which is translated in many instances "ask." It means to ask or to question something, to interrogate. But it is asking on an equal basis, not as an inferior to a superior. Let me give you a verse in which both of these words occur, so that you can understand the important distinction between them. It is John 16:23, which I will translate directly from the Greek text. Our Lord is speaking to His disciples, and in the first part of the verse He says, "And in that day you will not ask me anything." The word there for "ask" is *erooteesete,* not the word used in Luke 11:9. The translation should have been, "And in that day you shall interrogate me about nothing." Of course, it will not be necessary to interrogate the Lord about anything in that day because everything will be made plain. And John 16:23 continues, "Verily, verily [Amen, amen], I say unto you, that whatsoever ye shall ask the Father in my name, he will give it you." The word "ask" there is the same as the one we find in Luke 11:9, *aiteeseete,* "ask as beggars." You must submit yourself as if you were a beggar coming to a king to ask for something. "If you shall ask," *coming, not demanding.* No beggar can demand anything. Beggars cannot be choosers. "Then my Father will give it unto you." Thus we understand

110

the word "ask" in Luke 11:9 means to come with respect, to ask as if we were beggars.

Jesus Prayed As Being Equal with the Father

It's interesting to note that whenever the Lord is praying to His Father, either on His own behalf or on behalf of others, He never uses this word *aiteoo,* but always *erootaoo,* the word that would put Him on an equal level with the Father. This is extremely important. Some people ask, "Did the Lord ever claim equality with God?" Of course, He did. The very fact that when He asks us to pray, He tells us to ask like beggars; but whenever He prays to the Father, He prays on a basis of equality, demonstrates this. His is not the petition of the creature to the Creator, but the request of the Son to the Father. The consciousness of His equality, the equal dignity of His potent and prevailing intercession, speaks out in this — that as often as He asks or declares that He will ask anything of the Father, the word "ask" is always *erootaoo,* asking that is upon equal terms. In John 14:16; 16:26; 17:9, 16, 20, the Lord also uses the verb *erootaoo,* bringing Him on an equal basis with the Father. It takes a knowledge of the Greek New Testament to realize this.

Our Lord said, "And I, myself, say unto you intelligently, ask." The verb is in the plural form here, not singular — *aiteite.* Why is it plural? Because the Lord wants us all to ask collectively and individually. There isn't a single one of us who is excluded from this, because we are all His creatures and He is our Creator and Sustainer.

You know, there is nothing more simple than asking. That's what prayer is. The other day I read a true story that touched my heart, and I would like to share it with you.

111

The Story of "Jim" and His "Visitor"

The vicar of a certain church hurried to the cottage where his church caretaker lived. "I'm worried," he explained. "Every day at noon a shabby old man goes into the church. I can see him through the vicarage window. He only stays a few minutes. It seems most mysterious and you know the altar furnishings are quite valuable. I wish you would keep an eye open and question the fellow."

The next day, and so for many days, the caretaker watched and sure enough, at noon the shabby figure would arrive. One day the caretaker accosted him. "Look here, my friend, what are you up to going into the church every day?"

"I go to pray," the old man replied quietly.

"Now come," the caretaker said sternly. "You don't stay long enough to pray. You're only there a few minutes. I have watched you. You just go up to the altar every day and then come away."

"Yes, that's true; I cannot pray a long prayer. But every day at 12 o'clock I just come and say, 'Jesus, it's Jim,' then I wait a minute and then come away. It's just a little prayer, but I guess He hears me."

Sometime later poor Jim was knocked down by a car and was taken to the city hospital where he settled down quite happily while his broken leg mended. The ward where Jim lay had been a sore spot to the doctors and nurses for a long time. Some of the men were cross and miserable. Others did nothing but grumble from morning till night. Try as she would, the Sister on that ward could do nothing to improve the situation.

Then slowly but surely things changed. The men stopped grumbling and were cheerful and contented. They took their medicine, ate their food, and settled down without a complaint.

One day, hearing the burst of happy laughter, the Sister

asked, "What has happened to you all? You are such a nice, cheerful lot of patients now. Where have all the grumbles gone?"

"Oh, it's old Jim," one patient replied. "He's always so happy and never complains, although we know he must be in a lot of pain. He makes us ashamed to make a murmur. Now, we can't grumble when Jim's about. He is always so cheerful."

Sister crossed over to where Jim lay. His silvery hair gave him an angelic look. His quiet eyes were full of peace. "Well, Jim," Sister greeted him, "the men say you are responsible for the change in this ward. They say you are always happy."

"Oh, yes, Sister, that I am. I can't help being happy. You see, Sister, it's my Visitor. Every day He makes me happy."

"Your visitor?" The Sister was puzzled. She had noticed that Jim's chair was always empty on visiting days, for he was a lonely old man without any relations. "Your visitor?" she asked. "But, when does He come?"

"Every day," Jim replied, the light in his eyes growing brighter. "Yes, every day at noon He comes and stands at the foot of my bed I see Him and He smiles and says, 'Jim, it's Jesus.' "

You know, that's asking and receiving. When you say, "Lord, I'm here," He says, "Jim, I'm here." That's prayer. The Lord couldn't put it in any simpler way. He says, "Ask, and it shall be given unto you."

A Submissive Spirit in Prayer

Now, the interesting thing is that the verb *dotheesetai* in Greek, "it shall be given unto you," has the connotation that you will not grasp, but it's up to God to give to you. You ask as if you were a beggar, and beggars don't demand things, they just make their requests known. Ask in that way and you will receive something.

Our Lord is teaching us here that if we come to Him with a spirit of humility as if we were beggars, and not playing the part of God, we shall always receive something when we ask. We are to keep on asking, and He will keep on giving us what is best for us, and that's the best thing that could happen to us.

THINK IT OVER

1. What does the Greek word *aiteoo* indicate about our attitude in prayer?
2. What does the Greek word *erootaoo* indicate about how the Lord Jesus came to the Father in prayer?
3. With what attitude do you pray — as one who "requests" or one who "demands"?

20

"SEEK AND KNOCK"

Now we come to the word "seek," *zeeteite,* in Greek. What does this word actually mean? Seek, *zeeteoo* (nominative, first person singular) is the Greek word.

Jesus Seeks the Lost

When used in a religious sense, this word first denotes the seeking of what is lost, which is undertaken by the Son of man with a view to saving it, as in Luke 19:10: "For the Son of man is come to seek and to save that which was lost." It means to find that which actually belongs to Him but is wandering far away from Him. He came to seek that which belongs to Him, as a shepherd looks for the lost sheep in Matthew 18:12, or as a woman looks for a lost coin in Luke 15:8.

God Seeks Fruit, Faithfulness, True Worship

It is also used of the holy demand of God who requires much from him to whom much is given (Luke 12:48), and who expects fruit from the tree as indicated in Luke 13:6. He demands, He is looking for, He seeks faithfulness from His stewards (I Cor. 4:2). He is asking worship in spirit and in truth by the truly righteous (John 4:23).

Man Seeks God Himself

The Lord Jesus seeks because of His claim to what belongs to Him. But, when the word *zeeteoo* is used by man as man's requirement, it does not have the ring of pitiless rigor but rather of patient and hopeful expectation. So faith asks, but asks on behalf of a beggar from an omniscient God. Therefore he cannot demand what he wants, but is to be satisfied with what God chooses to give him. In the word "seek," *zeeteoo*, there is the thought of patient and hopeful expectation. We come to God as a beggar and then we wait. We expect Him to do something about our petition. And God will always honor His promises.

It's very suggestive that the second clause, *zeeteite kai evreesete,* "seek, and ye shall find," means "you seek and you shall find on your own." I believe that this refers to God Himself as the object of our seeking. If we seek God, we will find Him on our own. But as in the story of the prodigal son who came to his father, and his father ran to meet him, when God knows that we are seeking Him, He will come to meet us. He's eager and waiting for us to meet Him.

Seeking is almost as easy as asking. A little more difficult, perhaps, but God promises to help us with the finding. Knocking is not difficult, it is easy. So prayer is the easiest thing in the world: "Ask, seek, knock."

Seeking and Finding — a Favorite Theme of Scripture

Jesus Himself was a seeker. He came "to seek and to save

that which was lost." His parables, His teachings, are full of seeking and finding. He liked to speak of people who seek until they find. And we have illustration after illustration in the Word of God of those who sought and found. The merchant, for instance, sought for goodly pearls. The midnight caller found a friend, and that friend sought help for him from a neighbor. And then in Luke 18:2-8 we find the woman who came to the judge and persisted until he heard her cry and did something about it.

The Kingdom of Heaven is like treasure hidden in a field. The Lord finds faith in a Roman soldier. He finds faith in heathen women. He finds lost womanhood in the Samaritan woman at the well. He seeks and finds generosity in that tight person called Zacchaeus. He seeks and finds courage in Peter, that coward who wouldn't reveal even to a little maid who he was while Jesus was being tried. The Lord seeks and finds an Apostle in a persecutor like Saul of Tarsus and makes him Paul.

Seeking Is a Challenge to Plumb the Depths of God

The Lord didn't tell people who He was. Oh, no! He gave them only hints and helps. He wanted them to seek and find out for themselves who He was.

Be a seeker. You cannot find the depths of God unless you seek God out and plumb these depths. The trouble with most people is that they are not seekers of the Word of God and of the riches of God. Like the disciples, we must ask, "Lord, teach us to pray," and then learn from the Word what it is that we are to seek from Him.

What God Promises to Give to Those Who Seek His Will

Sometimes God doesn't give us what we ask for, because

we ask amiss. It is a good thing He doesn't, in many cases. If God gave us all that we asked for, we could easily be the most miserable creatures on earth, because sometimes we misjudge our needs.

Suppose I conceive a great desire for money, and ask God, "Make me rich!" How do I know that this would be for my good or for my ruin? There is no promise in Scripture that if the Christian asks for riches God will give them to him. It is "our daily bread" that is to be asked for, our needs. In the parable of the midnight caller, he was given only what was needed to satisfy the hunger of his friend — bread. Necessities are what God promises to fulfill and give, a sufficiency to carry us through this life as long as God is pleased to keep us in it. We pray subject to our Father's judgment as to what is really good for us.

God Looks Upon Us as Personalities Related to Him

This word of Christ signifies that God's mind and heart are fixed upon our case — not our particular demands, but upon us. It is a good thing that God does not look primarily at the things we need, but He looks upon us as personalities, and our relationship to Him. We must come to Him as having nothing and deserving nothing. But we can ask for all things. There are no limitations if we have the Spirit of God, for then we shall know what to ask.

Prayers We Know God Will Answer

What are those things that we are sure God wants us to ask for? First, the kingdom of God and His righteousness: "Seek ye first the kingdom of God, and his righteousness; and all these things shall be added unto you" (Matt. 6:33). What are "all these things"? What we desire? No! What God believes is necessary so that we may maintain our spiritual balance. We are to "seek those things which are above" (Col. 3:1); "Seek to be justified by Christ" (Gal. 2:17). We must always seek repentance (Mark 2:17).

Knock, knock at the door, the Lord says. As believers, we must realize that there is no wide-open door into which we can storm. Politeness is enjoined here. You don't open the door and go rushing in to the office of an important person. You knock first. Like a beggar we come to God expectantly seeking, and then politely knocking. Believers must seek access. Even the Lord respects our own hearts and knocks at our doors asking us to open so that He can come in and talk with us.

Now note the 10th verse: "Every one that asketh receiveth." Those verbs are in the continuous tense — "keeps on asking, keeps on receiving." And he who keeps on seeking keeps on finding, and he who keeps on knocking will have the door continuously opening to him. That is the message of this verse.

THINK IT OVER

1. Why does Christ want us to "seek" God; why not simply give us all the answers as soon as we ask?
2. What is God seeking from us?
3. Give several Scriptural examples of seeking and finding.
4. What does Scripture tell us to "seek"? List three things God wants us to ask for of a spiritual nature.

21

"BREAD, FISH, AND AN EGG" — COMMON THINGS WITH SACRED MEANINGS

From the 9th to the 26th verses of Luke 11 we find teachings about man, God, and the devils. Let's take a review and an overview of all that we find in this section of the Word of God. Then we will come back and study in greater depth and detail every important word in this section. (See forthcoming volumes.)

Soon after the parable of the midnight friend, with its teaching on prayer, the Lord Jesus added, "And I say unto you, Ask, and it shall be given you; seek, and ye shall find; knock, and it shall be opened unto you. For every one that asketh receiveth; and he that seeketh findeth; and to him that knocketh it shall be opened."

Earthly Versus Heavenly Fatherhood

To enforce the exhortation, the Lord then made a comparison between earthly fathers and the Heavenly Father, in the matter of asking and giving. It is another of His "How Much More" parables. "If a son shall ask bread of any of you that is a father, will he give him a stone? or if he ask a fish, will he for a fish give him a serpent? or if he shall ask an egg, will he offer him a scorpion?" (Luke 11:11, 12).

He then continued with this comparison: "If ye then, being evil, know how to give good gifts unto your children: how much more shall your heavenly Father give the Holy Spirit to them that ask him?"

Here you have two givers: one earthly, the other Heavenly. No earthly father, though wicked, would mock his needy child by giving stones instead of bread, a serpent instead of fish, or a scorpion instead of an egg. Don't take offense at God for calling us earthly fathers "evil." "For all have sinned, and come short of the glory of God" (Rom. 3:23). Our goodness when compared to the goodness and mercy of God is nothing but evil. What the Lord is saying here is, "If you, being of such lower moral caliber, do not mock your children by giving them something that will harm them, how much more will your Father be careful when you ask Him to give you something that He knows is for your good?"

This is a wonderful teaching, indicating that we can trust God as being not only a Father, as we might conceive the best earthly father to be, but far more than that — God Himself, the personification of goodness, who will never mock us. The most that an earthly father can give is bread, fish, and egg — symbolic of the various needs and requests of a son. But the Heavenly Father will give over and above all needful material things the supreme gift, the Holy Spirit. Jesus teaches us that one who receives the Holy Spirit has the key to all his needs, for he will know what is really necessary for himself and how to ask, seek, and knock.

God's Supreme Gift in Answer to Prayer

Observe the order of the teaching of our Lord here. He gives us the liberty first to ask, to seek, and to knock. And when we have asked, the Lord will never give us anything that will harm us. He will give what is for our eternal good — the Holy Spirit.

What does that mean? It means that He will indwell our hearts, and when you and I, indwelt by the Spirit of God, ask God for something, it is the Holy Spirit within us that asks Him. Therefore we can only ask Him for that which is consistent with His character.

Everyone, of course, understands what bread, fish, and eggs are. But not everyone realizes that these three things are also symbols of spiritual gifts. Bread, for instance, symbolizes life, a life nourished by the Spirit of God, which becomes fruitful in His service.

Symbols of Evil

Also everyone knows what a stone, a serpent, and a scorpion are. But in them we also see three symbols of delusion and evil. A stone in itself is innocuous. It is needed in constructing buildings, but it cannot be used as food. It may resemble bread, but if we touch it, it proves a delusion. The serpent with its venom, and the scorpion with its poisonous sting, are also dreadful pictures of evil.

Mere natural gifts are given by an earthly father. Heavenly gifts, summed up in the gift of the Holy Spirit, are bestowed by the Heavenly Father.

The Scriptures do not extend the comparison, but by what follows in the same chapter we discover that there are people who offer something resembling bread, and after the victim has been weakened by delusion he will be attacked and poisoned by serpents and scorpions. The Lord never left His Church without information on the forces and snares of evil. He has come to deliver us from darkness and from Satan and to bring us into light and love and the realm of the Son of God.

Though Matthew and Luke mention the bread and the fish, Luke alone adds the third section of the question, which asks for an egg to eat with the bread, and mentions a dead scorpion as the evil substitute — a poisonous creature, curled up, that was never eaten after it had been killed. Let us go a little deeper into what is meant by the word bread (*arton* in Greek). It was a small flat cake of wheat or barley flour, which resembled a stone. You remember when our Lord was tempted in the desert that Satan asked Him to turn the stones to bread. Why? Because bread and stones resembled each other: small, flat, and round. The bread of that day was not a large loaf as we understand it, but a single portion, like a flat bun. A son would not ask for a large loaf, which he could not consume, but for such a small flat cake of bread. The illustration, of course, is intensified by the addition of two more points. Fish in Galilee were the common addition to bread. A snake may resemble a fish, but is unfit to eat. The idea of harmfulness is not implied here, for certainly the snake could not be alive. The point lies in the deception attempted by such a father, which would reduce his fatherhood, and thereby the sonship of his innocent and trusting child, to an illusion.

Jesus, a Real Man, Using Common Things, and Teaching from Everyday Life

It's a very touching thought that our Lord was as familiar as we are with the common things of life. It gives a feeling of sacredness to them when we know that He mentioned them in His discourses or used them in His experience. Bread, fish, and an egg. How much more interesting a common egg becomes when we remember that just as we have eaten one at a meal our Savior did the same. It seems to bring the Lord very near to us, doesn't it? We see Him as a very real human being. And it helps to lift our common life into a kind of sacrament in which the life that we live in the flesh becomes a life of faith in the Son of God.

Luke 11:11 and 12 show us how keen was the interest that the Lord Jesus took in common things, how nothing belonging to the ordinary life of human beings was beneath His notice. He found everything full of instruction and suggestive of higher things. He connected in a kind of parable a common egg with the greatest mysteries of our religion, so that we cannot see an egg or partake of one without being reminded at the same time of the cord that binds our soul to God by prayer.

It is a good thing to have these Holy associations with homely things. It makes our religion not the thing of the Church only or of a practice of worship on Sunday, but also of the home and everyday life. Everything preaches to us and becomes a parable reminding us of the Kingdom of Heaven.

Prayer — Not a Form of Words but an Outpouring from the Heart to the Father

Our Lord was speaking to the disciples about prayer, which though so familiar to us was somewhat strange to them. The Jewish religion consisted mostly of rites and ceremonies offered to a God who was "afar off" and who kept everyone at a distance from Him by His awful holiness. The religionists of that day had not learned to know and love Him as their Father and therefore their hearts were not drawn out in longings after Him. The way of approach to Him in spirit was not opened and therefore prayer was a mere formal ceremony, consisting of certain fixed words uttered at stated times. The request of the disciples, "Lord, teach us to pray," meant for them "Give us a form and some directions that we may perform the duty in a proper way." But the Lord Jesus showed them that prayer was something quite different from that — that it was the free, full outpouring of the soul before God, the very spray, as it were, of excited emotion mounting up to Heaven from some real necessity. He taught them that prayer was not a question of kneeling, but of feeling. And it was an answer to the soul rather than to the form of their request.

He gave a beautiful and simple lesson on prayer. They were children in regard to this new instruction, and as a mother teaches her child to pray so did our Lord teach His disciples. And that first lesson which He gave they needed to refer to all their lives. And you and I need to keep it in mind continually.

Pray for Necessities, Not Luxuries

In explaining the lesson, the Lord Jesus used three illustrations taken from bread, fish, and an egg — articles of food that were in common use in those days. The provision carried by the lad who followed the Lord Jesus, along with the multitude, into the desert of Capernaum was five loaves and two fishes. That was the common food of that day. Of course, the bread, composed of small barley cakes baked at home, could be had anywhere throughout the Holy Land. But the fish could only come from the Sea of Galilee, where it formed part of the ordinary food of the people living upon the shores of the lake. The addition of the fish to the bread in our Lord's lesson marks out to us the locality where it was spoken.

How many times I have personally traveled in the Holy Land, and if I stayed with a family, they would pack a lunch for me consisting of bread, fried fish, and a couple of eggs. And the fact that the Lord Jesus compared the things for which we are to ask in prayer to these common everyday articles of food shows us that it is not changing luxuries or fanciful things for which we have an unreasonable desire that we are to ask of God, but for the necessities of life — the things that we cannot do without and that are the same to all men at all times.

How the words "ask, seek, knock" can be misunderstood. We feel we can ask for anything, but don't forget that immediately after these words the Lord says, "If a son ask his father for bread, for fish, for an egg" — the simple necessities of life, implying that when we come to God we should be content to ask God for what is necessary instead of for luxuries. Don't blame God for not keeping His word when He doesn't give you everything you ask for. He has promised you life's necessities. Trust Him to know what is best for you.

THINK IT OVER

1. What is the comparison Jesus makes between earthly and Heavenly Fatherhood in the matter of giving?
2. What is God's supreme gift that is ours for the asking?
3. How does receiving this gift affect our asking in prayer?
4. Of what are bread, fish, and an egg the symbol? Of what are a stone, a serpent, and a scorpion the symbol?
5. How may these be compared with what religionists today are offering us?

22

WHEN IS AN "EGG" NOT AN "EGG"?

Let's give our attention for a little while to the egg. I find something peculiarly fascinating and suggestive about our Lord's words, "If he shall ask an egg, will he offer him a scorpion?" It would seem that this was a familiar proverb among the Jews; the Greeks had a somewhat similar expression, "for a perch a scorpion."

Our Lord was well acquainted with the proverbs current among the common people and He often made use of them to give a familiar point to His own higher teaching. The lesson He intended to bring out of this proverb was that God would not mock the disciples by giving them an answer to their prayers that bore a deceptive resemblance to the thing asked for, but which would only cause disappointment or harm when the deception was discovered.

God Never Mocks Us by Playing Practical Jokes

A scorpion is an ugly, venomous creature like a small crab — found in hot climates under stones and among ruins — with a poisonous sting in its tail that causes a very painful wound. It would be a very cruel thing to give a horrid beast

129

like that to one who was hungry and wanted an egg. Some senseless persons without any imagination might indeed consider this a practical joke. We have heard of mischievous young men throwing out red-hot pennies to children in order to enjoy the "fun" of hearing the poor creatures shrieking with pain when they eagerly clutched them from the ground; or giving red pepper pods to children, telling them they were good to eat, that they might see the tears of pain starting up as the vegetable flame burned their tender mouths. Thoughtless persons have often played cruel tricks like these and it is no uncommon thing for young people at school to get a rise out of their innocent companions by such abominable deceptions.

The Natural Instincts of Parents to Children Prompt Them to Give What Is Good for Them

But, apart from bestial child abusers, you cannot fancy a natural father doing anything of that kind to his own son. Our Lord said that, however selfish human nature might be, however evil parents might be in themselves, their natural instincts prompted them to give good things to their children. Most of us know from experience that our fathers could not by any possibility have given us things fraught with deadly harm. And Christ reasons from this common instinct of our nature that has passed into a proverb because of its very commonness.

Trust in God's Father-Heart to Give Only What Is Best

But He who made the father's heart has a Father's heart in His own bosom and will surely give good gifts and only good gifts to His praying children. It might seem indeed to the disciples as if, when they had asked for a thing on which their hearts were very much set — that is to say the restoration of the Jewish Kingdom and their own appointment to positions of honor and authority — that God had grievously disappointed their expectations, as if He had given them a scorpion for an egg.

Why Weren't the Disciples' Prayers Answered as They Expected?

You remember that the disciples came one day to Jesus and asked for the establishment of His literal Kingdom on earth. They also said, "Master, we would like some special positions in Thy Kingdom." Why didn't they get what they asked for? Hadn't the Lord told them to "ask, and it shall be given unto you"? Yes, but then He said that if you are a son and ask your father for bread, for fish, or an egg — the necessities of life — these are the things He would supply. But the disciples were asking for great positions in an imposed political kingdom. Did the Lord disappoint them? Very much so. They probably felt that He had given them a "scorpion," a deceptive fulfillment of His promise. Christ crucified on the cross was not what they had envisioned at all. The egg of hope that their fond imagination had been hatching brought forth the scorpion of the cross to their Master, and shame and persecution to themselves. But afterwards, when their eyes were opened by the Holy Spirit, they saw that all that Christ had promised them had been fulfilled, that God had indeed given them what they had asked, and in a higher and more lasting form than that which they had expected.

Similarly, all who ask God in earnest prayer, and leave the choice to Him, will find out that the answers to their prayers are truly answers and not deceptions — that when they ask for an egg, they get an egg.

Our Values Not Always God's Values

When we ask for health and the Lord gives us sickness, we are not to think He is giving us a scorpion. If at any time the Hearer of prayer seems to deal with us in a cruel manner, we may be sure it is because we have made a mistake about the nature of the good thing we wanted. We place the wrong values on things. We think that health, fame, a successful career, and prosperity are the things that are going to be most beneficial to us. But God doesn't think so sometimes, and in our disappointment we complain, "I asked my Father for an egg and He gave me a scorpion."

All Eggs are Not Good Eggs

There are eggs and eggs, you know. All eggs are not good and wholesome. The egg of the hen is not unlike that of some types of serpents' eggs in appearance. And very often people ask for a serpent's egg thinking it to be a hen's egg. They ask for health and prosperity, but that may only drive them away from God. Rather than helping them it might harm them. The prayers of people, unknown to themselves, are often similar to what the prophet Isaiah said of people who hatched eggs which turned out to be cockatrices' (adders') eggs, containing venomous serpents. "He that eateth of their eggs dieth, and that which is crushed breaketh out into a viper" (Isa. 59:5). How true it is that we do not know what to pray for as we ought. People are constantly mistaking what is good for them, and asking God for things for which, if they were granted, they would curse Him. The teaching is obvious, that we must be sure that it is a real egg that we ask for; not what we take to be an egg, but the genuine article.

Letting God Choose What Is Best for Us

But how can we be sure of this? We are ignorant, short-sighted, and easily deceived by appearances. And we are certainly liable to make mistakes as to what is good for us, imagining that if we get certain things that appear to us to be good, and upon which our heart is set, they cannot but be really good, whereas, they may turn out to be serpents' eggs. The best way, then, is to leave the matter entirely in God's hands and ask Him to judge for us what is best. He has bestowed upon us His unspeakable Gift, His beloved Son, and with that He has given us a guarantee that He will not withhold from us any good thing.

132

Literal Answers to Prayer Not Always Best

Young people are intense realists, prone to construe everything literally. As the French say, "With all its feet on the ground." If they ask for an egg they expect to get an egg and nothing else. Because of this they are often laying up disappointments for themselves, owing to this immature concept of prayer. For instance, I have known of a child praying to God that his little brother might be made well, but the brother died. The child in his grief and sore disappointment said to his mother, "There's no use in praying any more for God to give people what they want." And I have heard a boy complaining bitterly that he had prayed to God that the next day might be a fine day so that he could go to an outdoor amusement park on which he was very much set. Because it turned out to be a miserably wet day, and he had to stay at home, he felt like one who had asked God for an egg and been given a scorpion, and he lost all faith in prayer.

Bring Everything to God and Leave the Answers to His Wisdom

In all of this, there was no consideration of seeking God's will, or of accepting what God knew to be best. Subject to that stipulation, it is our happy privilege to tell God everything. We are His little children and we need not be afraid to trust our wants to Him. The trouble is, we sometimes ask for what we think is an egg, and God is good enough to refuse us because He knows it is not an egg at all, but something that will hurt us.

What If We Ask for the Wrong Things?

But even if we make a mistake in our asking, God will not deal with us harshly, although He may say to us, "Ye know not what ye ask" (Mark 10:38). That is what Jesus told the disciples when they asked for positions of prominence in an earthly kingdom. "You don't know what you ask for when you ask for fame, when you ask Me to exercise My strength instead of My love," was what He meant. We can be very sure of this, that even if we make a mistake in praying for something we suppose is good, our Heavenly Father will not give us a "scorpion" to sting us in answer to our prayer. Let's not be afraid to make a mistake when we pray, for we can be comforted by the thought that our Lord is not going to heed us in such a case, but will give us that which He knows is best instead of what we think is good for us.

Reasssurance of Divine Help in Our Prayers

Romans 8:26 is a most reassuring verse to rely on when we pray: "Likewise the Spirit also helpeth our infirmities: for we know not what we should pray for as we ought: but the Spirit itself maketh intercession for us with groanings which cannot be uttered." Quite often we don't know how to pray or what to pray for. But if we have the Holy Spirit within us, we shall come to know better. We may be very sure of this, that whatever happens, our Heavenly Father will not give us anything harmful in answer to our prayers.

Why We Don't Always Recognize God's Answers to Our Prayers

However, the egg for which we ask may be given to us in a different form from that which we expect. We do not always get it as a hard, white oval with shell on it so that we can recognize it at once. It may take on many appearances, even as it does in ordinary preparation for human nourishment. It may be cooked and served in many dishes, as an egg salad, a scrambled, boiled, or fried egg, or incorporated in a cake or pudding. Yet it is the real, genuine egg after all, even if there be no empty shells visible to tell us the origin of what we get.

An egg is for two purposes: to be eaten and to produce a chicken that in due time will lay many eggs. There are many things in life that are best not to be consumed for the satisfaction of the moment, but which should be allowed to grow into future blessings far more precious and enduring.

And sometimes God gives us an answer to our prayer that is not for the moment, but for the future, not for the satisfaction of a pressing want, but for the lasting good of our souls.

The Best and Most Satisfying Answer to Prayer — God's Peace

The Apostle Paul says, "In every thing by prayer and supplication with thanksgiving let your request be made known unto God" (Phil. 4:6). Will they be granted just as we wish or expect? Not necessarily. What does he go on to say? "And the peace of God, which passeth all understanding, shall keep your hearts and minds through Christ Jesus" (v. 7). That is the answer that God always gives. That is the form in which the egg is immediately bestowed upon us. That is the one answer we may be sure of getting at all times and in all circumstances. If we pray earnestly to God, whatever may be the answer, the peace of God will keep our hearts and minds. And the answer of peace, begetting a patience, a gentleness, a strength before unknown, will more than compensate us for the loss of a literal answer.

For instance, if we pray for a fine day in which to enjoy our play, but the day turns out wet, yet we are made contented and happy otherwise, that may be as real an answer to our prayer as if God had granted it literally. For what we wanted the fine day for was to be made happy, and if we can be made happy otherwise, the same end is gained. If we pray that a sick brother may be made well, and God makes him well indeed by taking him to a place where the inhabitants will no longer say, "I am sick," and at the same time makes us better prepared to follow him in due time, does He not answer our prayer in even a better way than if He had restored our brother here?

THINK IT OVER

1. How did the Lord Jesus qualify His promise, "Ask, and it shall be given unto you," in a way that would limit what we should ask for and expect from the Father?
2. How can we have confidence that our mistaken requests will not bring answers that will harm us? (See Rom. 8:26.)
3. If we pray about everything in the right spirit, what one answer can we always be sure of getting? (See Phil. 4:6, 7.)
4. When is an "egg" not an "egg"?

23

GOD: THE ALL GOOD AND ALL KNOWING FATHER, WHO WILL NEVER DECEIVE US

When the Apostle Paul prayed three times that the thorn in his flesh might be removed, and it was not, don't you think the answer he got, "My grace is sufficient for thee" (II Cor. 12:9), was a far better thing than if the thorn had been actually taken away? Of course it was; for the removal of the thorn would have been a temporary relief, leaving behind no abiding results, and would have been a blessing to Paul alone. (Sometimes when we ask God to do something in our lives we only have ourselves in mind. But God has in mind the whole of humanity.) The answer God bestowed gave Paul comfort all the days of his life, and has been a source of unspeakable comfort to all believers ever since. We know that for these reasons Paul was perfectly satisfied with it, for he said, "Most gladly therefore will I rather glory in my infirmities, that the power of Christ may rest upon me."

Our Savior Himself prayed three times for what could not be given to Him. And when he asked an "egg," a seeming scorpion was offered — the cup from which He shrank with dread in Gethsemane. But He got God's best answer when He yielded His will, saying, "Father...not my will, but thine be done" (Luke 22:42), and an angel came and strengthened Him (v. 43). He knew that the agony which He endured would be the salvation of the world.

Our Unanswered Prayers Work Together for Our Good

In like manner the time will come for all of us when we shall see clearly that our wise and loving Father has been making even our unanswered prayers work together for our good, and has thus answered them in reality. In the best way, He has given us the true egg for which we really, unknown to ourselves, hungered and longed.

However, it is well to remember that our parents cannot give us an egg without toil and trouble. The farmer's wife had to feed the hens day after day, and go out to the barn to get the newly laid egg, before she could give it to her child to eat. If a son had asked his father for an egg in Jerusalem in Jesus' day, the father or mother would have had to go outside the walls of the city to some neighboring village, such as Bethany, to buy it with hard-earned money, for no hens were allowed to be kept in the sacred city lest they pollute it.

Our Part in Securing Answers to Prayer

Even so, God, our Heavenly Father, cannot give us the egg of an answered prayer without toil and patience on our part. Our Heavenly Father knows it would not do us any good if we always got an answer to our prayers as if by magic, without any self-sacrifice or trouble to ourselves. So when the Lord says, "Ask, and it shall be given you," it is not a promise that everything we ask for will just drop in our laps. We have to work for some things. Remember the admonition, "Work out your own salvation..." (Phil. 2:12). Of course, salvation is a free gift of God. We don't earn it. But the outworking of it in daily practical life is our responsibility, in obedience to God's will, as revealed in His Word.

In my book on James, I have a couple of chapters on the deserved mercies of the believer, when he obeys God and does something about the circumstances of his life and the lives of others. Sometimes if we want an egg, we have to strive for it. The egg in that case would most surely hatch, and, if it is well taken care of, will most likely produce a hen that will multiply eggs from which to feed our hunger. We must create this hunger by earning it, by exercising ourselves unto Godliness. We must get up an appetite for it by patient persevering effort in order to relish the egg truly when we get it.

Prayer is not always effective at once. The answer to it is sometimes slow in coming. The force of it is accumulative; the egg has to grow, to be formed from the smallest beginning to have its materials collected and prepared, before it can be given to us. And we ourselves must be prepared to enjoy and digest the egg so that it may become part of our being and build up our life.

God's Giving Far Greater than Human Giving

In Luke 11:13 our Lord says, "If ye then [we human beings], being evil, know how to give good gifts unto your children; how much more shall your Heavenly Father give...?" As I've said, this is one of the "How much more parables." "...how much more shall your heavenly Father give the Holy Spirit to them that ask him?" The argument here is from the less to the greater and it is answerable. If the human father whose love is only partial, whose knowledge is only partial, whose morality is only relative, knows how to give good gifts, how much more does your Heavenly Father know? It clinches all that precedes it regarding the assurance that our prayers to our Father will be heard. As earthly fathers prove their fatherhood by giving good gifts to their children, so our Heavenly Father proves that he is indeed our Father and we are indeed His children, by giving to us in answer to our asking in our time of need.

And what are these answers to our prayers? The word here is "good gifts," *agatha* in Greek. This is a beautiful word. It means beneficial things, "good things" as Matthew 7:11 has it or "the Holy Spirit," as Luke has it (Luke 11:13). These are parallel passages of Scripture.

Look at Matthew 7:11: "If ye then, being evil, know how to give good gifts unto your children [in Greek it is two words here, *domata agatha,* beneficial gifts], how much more shall your Father which is in heaven give good things [the same word, *agatha* without the word *domata* — gifts] to them that ask him?"

Now look at Luke 11:13: "If ye then, being evil, know how to give good gifts unto your children [the same words *domata agatha*]; how much more shall your heavenly Father give...?" What? Luke summarizes all good things that come from God in one single item, "the Holy Spirit." We ask Him for good gifts, and He gives us the Holy Spirit. Oh, maybe we ask for a particular thing, thinking it is an egg, thinking it is bread, thinking it is fish, and the Lord instead gives us the Holy Spirit, through whom we have all things.

Our Limitations Contrasted with God's Perfection

Our Lord says to His disciples and to us, "If ye, then, being evil . . . ." The word "evil" there in the Greek New Testament is *poneeroi*. There are actually three words that can be translated evil in Greek: *kakos, poneeros,* and *phaulos*. When three

140

words are translated by one word, it is difficult for the reader to know which one is meant. And there is a difference between these words. The word that is used here, *poneeros,* can be contrasted to *kakos. Poneeros* means not only the one who is evil in himself, but who also propagates that evil. That is why, as I said before, the devil is called *poneeros,* "the evil one," because the devil is not satisfied with being evil in himself, but is trying to propagate that evil to make others like himself.

Now why did the Lord use the word *poneeroi* (masculine plural of *poneeros*) here instead of *kakoi* (masculine plural of *kakos*)? In other words why did He say that sometimes in the exercise of our fatherly duties we are not only evil in ourselves but are also trying to spread evil to others? I believe He wanted here to contrast our limitations with God's perfection. A father can be evil and even harm his children. But God can never be an evil father and God can never propagate evil.

You remember (in Matthew 19) that the rich young ruler came to our Lord and called Him "Good Master." And the Lord said, in effect, "Don't call me good; only God is good (*agathos*)." Now why did He say that? It was because He wanted to show him that goodness is really acceptable in its ultimate analysis only if it is the quality that pertains to God. Our goodness is only partial goodness, and therefore we may commit evil at times without realizing it. But that is impossible with God. That is the difference between an earthly father and our Father in Heaven. An earthly father can indeed do evil to his children, but God will never do this, for His goodness is perfect.

Isn't it true that we fathers give in to our children sometimes to the extent of spoiling them and thus destroying their moral character? But the Lord Jesus tells us in Luke 11:13 that it is impossible for God ever to do evil to us, or be evil in Himself, or even make a mistake in giving us that which we ought not to have.

For the most part a father takes care of his children, but there are times when he fails them because of the limitation of his goodness, because of the innate sin in every human heart. We are not perfect, but God is perfect, ultimate, complete, full goodness. And He will never, never do us any harm by what He chooses to give us.

God's Knowledge of What Is Good for Us Far Greater than Ours

Very interestingly the word "know" that is used here, "ye *know* how to give good gifts," is *oidate* in Greek, which means instinctive knowledge. A father doesn't have to learn how to give good gifts to his children. That is part and parcel of the instinctive knowledge of fatherhood. "If you *know* how to give good gifts to your children, how much more your Father who has come from heaven [that is actually what the Greek text says] will give . . . ." Luke 11:13 says, "He will give the Holy Spirit to those who seek him." Seek (not "ask") is the actual Greek word used here. It is *aitousin* (dative plural of *aiteoo*), which brings man on a lower level than God, like a beggar, as I explained earlier in this study. What the Lord is really telling us here is that God is the personification of goodness, in distinction to us who are evil.

Right Prayers Get Right Answers

The child in this parable is not represented as asking for a stone, but seeking as he should a most proper gift, namely bread. No mistake was made at all by the child. His prayer is what it should be. Prayers for good things will be answered, the Lord tells us, and they will not be answered with gifts wearing the mere appearance of good, but with the actual good things desired.

What the Lord is actually telling us here is that right prayers will get right answers. If we ask God for necessities, as symbolized by bread, he will give us "bread," not a stone that looks like it.

Fish at that time was not considered an absolute necessity, but more of a comfort and a relish. Well, God will give us so much of comfort as we can bear. As for the eating of eggs, here and in the Book of Job (and Job was a rich man), do we ever read anywhere else of the third item that is mentioned here? In fact, all through the Bible we find no mention of poultry till our Savior's day; and then chickens were so valuable that eggs were considered a luxury for which a child would hardly be expected to ask.

Necessity, Comfort, or Luxury — Which?

We have three steps here: necessity — bread; fish — comfort; egg — luxury. If we have asked God to guide us in all the steps of our life, we should look upon our present lot as from the Lord and accept it as such. He has not given us a stone. Maybe sometimes it looks hard, but that may be because the crust is hard. Underneath is the nourishment we need. We must never suspect under any circumstances that we are treated ungenerously by our Lord. He has given us that which is for our lasting good. Our present distress may appear evil, but it is not. Every circumstance of our affliction is made subservient to our souls' perfection. God will not deceive us, for He is innately good.

Salvation Guaranteed to the Truly Repentant

For instance, we will not be deceived in the matter of our

143

repentance. When we repent, the Lord has promised He will give us eternal life. He will make us taste of the things of Heaven. He will fill our hearts with joy. He will not disappoint us or deceive us in this matter.

This is taught in a very difficult passage of Scripture, Hebrews 6:4-6, which is often greatly misunderstood. In English it reads: "For it is impossible for those who were once enlightened, and have tasted ot the heavenly gift, and were made partakers of the Holy Ghost, and have tasted the good word of God, and the powers of the world to come, if they shall fall away, to renew them again unto repentance . . . ." Observe, "*if* they shall fall." It doesn't say that they *can* fall away. "If" they have tasted the Word of God, "if" they shall fall away. This is a hypothetical case.

Now the Greek word for "renew" in verse 6 means to have another kind of repentance that is effective — not of the same quality as you had before, which has failed you, if such a thing were possible. And in order to have a new kind of repentance which would not fail, it would be necessary to re-crucify Christ as verse 6 goes on to say, "seeing they crucify to themselves the Son of God afresh, and put him to an open shame." In other words, it is the dependability of the work of Christ on the cross that is spoken of here. Assume that a person has asked the Lord to save him and has repented of his sins. Now, if he truly repented, God is going to save him, and that repentance is going to prove that the work of grace is not a deception of God, but will carry him through to heaven. Isn't that wonderful? So the Lord will never deceive us. He is a good Heavenly Father.

144

THINK IT OVER

1. Why were the prayers of Paul and Jesus for deliverance from suffering not answered as they desired? In what sense were they truly answered?
2. Explain how Hebrews 6:4-6 teaches the impossibility of the truly repentant sinner ever losing his salvation.

24

THE HOLY SPIRIT — THE SUMMATION OF THE BEST THINGS IN LIFE

We have said it is impossible for God to deceive us in any way. But when we ask for something and He gives us something else, do we say in effect, "I asked for bread and He gave me a stone"? Or when He tells us to repent and we will become new creatures in Christ, do we begin to wonder, "Have I really become a new creature or not?"

Have a Firsthand Religion to Avoid Being Deceived

Now if we went to pretenders, to other human beings, and asked them to mediate between us and God, we would certainly be disappointed and realize we had been deceived. But if we come to God directly we will never be deceived. Remember, there can be no mediator between man and God except the Lord Jesus Christ. When we have a firsthand religion we won't be deceived. We must go directly to the Lord Jesus Christ, and His Spirit will be given to us. He will indwell us.

This whole matter of deception applies to our total Christian experience. Never mind if we have had no ecstasies.

Never mind if some people say, "In order to know that you are a Christian, you must begin to shout, you must have this ecstasy, you must have this vision, this particular experience." Not at all. The Lord's peace will dwell in our hearts for sure if we repent of our sins, and the Holy Spirit comes to indwell us.

Suffering Promised to Believers, along with God's Grace and Peace

Don't ever feel that God has deceived you. Unbelievers will say, "Isn't the whole Christian experience a sham? You have been deceived, man! Here you trusted Jesus Christ, and look at the suffering you are going through. That's not what Christianity promised." Don't believe those people. The Lord distinctly warns us, "In the world ye shall have tribulation" (John 16:33), but His peace abideth. Remember what God said to Paul? "My grace is sufficient for thee." We have no right to suspect that God has deceived us in any way.

Like a child I believe that my Heavenly Father has given me what I asked for. I have done right in so believing. My child would do me a gross injustice if he suspected that the fish I gave him was not a fish, but a serpent; and I do my God a great injustice, if sincerely knowing that I have sought the one thing needful at His hands through Jesus Christ, I suspected that He has permitted me to be deluded with something else. No, if I sought it from Him, I sought it sincerely, and I have now the good thing that I longed for.

Others will tell us that we have been deceived. Our faith is not real, they will say. We have a stone instead of bread. You know all Christianity is not a euphoric experience. It is a realistic way of life. Remember that you may have more of God in the suffering that He has permitted in your life than in the abundance of health. The prayer for the best thing is surest of an answer. The Lord will give us the Holy Spirit. Do you know how great a gift this is? There can be no better gift, because the Holy Spirit entering into us puts us in tune with

148

God Himself, and it is He who asks God on our behalf, and not we alone. The Holy Spirit is the embodiment of all good things. God will give them to us; no doubt about it. When we say in all sincerity, "Lord I believe," the Lord will give us the Holy Spirit to indwell us.

The Holy Spirit is sometimes represented as the wind. In fact, *pneuma* is the Greek word for spirit. It comes from the verb *pneoo,* from which we get *pneuma,* wind. It is like asking for the wind to blow, and the wind blows. It is the life-giving breath of God. The Holy Spirit is a person, one of the three persons of the Trinity. But He is the one who gives life-giving breath to the individual. The Holy Spirit is represented sometimes as water, because He purifies. He is represented sometimes as light, because He illumines the mind and makes natural darkness flee. God has given us His Son, and now the Holy Spirit, for this is the dispensation of the Holy Spirit. Before that, the Holy Spirit was "with" us, but now He is "in" us. The Holy Spirit is represented as fire, which kindles and fuses, and burns with zeal in us. He is represented as oil, for divine anointing, for the touch of God upon us. We are told to have our lamps supplied with oil, that our light may not go out, as in the parable of the virgins and their lamps. He is represented also as dropping dew, because He refreshes our spirits. The Holy Spirit is represented as a dove, as in the baptism of our Lord, when the Holy Spirit came upon Him in the form of a dove. When we pray to our Heavenly Father, we are to ask for the best, and the best is the Holy Spirit, who will be given to us.

Watch Out for Evil Spirits!

But sometimes people have been deceived by an evil spirit. Watch it! "Try the spirits," we are told in I John 4:1. These are the characteristics of the evil spirit: it makes us self-sufficient; it makes us feel important in ourselves; it makes us feel superior to others. One of the basic characteristics of the Holy Spirit is that He gives us humility.

The Holy Spirit is received in answer to prayer. We should never think we have Him once and for all and don't need a fresh infilling daily. Ephesians 5:18 says, "And be not drunk with wine, wherein is excess; but be filled with the Spirit." That word "be filled with the Spirit" does not have the connotation of a once-and-for all experience. *Pleerootheete* is not in the aorist tense, but it is *pleerousthe,* in the present imperfect passive tense, that expresses a continuous and repeated infilling of the Holy Spirit. The Holy Spirit comes within us when we are saved, but we need a constant infilling of the Holy Spirit: "be [continuously] filled with the Spirit."

Characteristics of the Infilling of the Holy Spirit

And then Paul goes on to give us some of the characteristics of the infilling of the Holy Spirit. In verse 19 he says, "Speaking to yourselves in psalms and hymns and spiritual songs, singing and making melody in your heart to the Lord." There will be rejoicing in the heart where the Holy Spirit dwells. He will put a new song in our mouth and in our heart. Verse 20 continues, "Giving thanks always for all things unto God and the Father in the name of our Lord Jesus Christ." We won't be grumblers if the Holy Spirit indwells us; we will be thanks-givers. And then observe verse 21, "Submitting yourselves one to another in the fear of God." There is no attitude of superiority or contempt toward others, but a spirit of real appreciation. And then verse 22, "Wives, submit yourselves unto your own husbands, as unto the Lord."

These are the signs, the results of the indwelling of the Holy Spirit. God will give us the Spirit, not merely some mistaken manifestation of it, such as an emotional enthusiasm that might mislead us, or fanaticism that might injure us, or self-conceit that might become like a deadly scorpion. No, the Holy Spirit will not give us any of these. In the Holy Spirit we will receive only good things, as Matthew 7:11 says.

Why Christians Are Still "Evil" Within

In Luke 11:13 we read, "If ye then, being evil. . ." The word "being" there is *huparchontes*, which refers to the basic nature of man. "If you in your nature being evil" — and the Lord was speaking to the disciples here! How could He call them evil? Well, you remember what the Apostle Paul said in the seventh chapter of Romans. He confessed to a period of depression, a period when the natural man has the upper hand. The natural man is still a part of the Christian's nature, and he is rotten. He is evil. He seeks to please Satan. But praise God, the Spirit of God also indwells the believer, and He gives the victory. Nevertheless, we must never forget that we are evil within, that we have the possibility of choosing evil instead of good. The Apostle Paul struggled and said in effect, "Alas, I don't do the thing that I know is best to do! I do the thing that is not good." Yes, we are evil and we have got to watch lest our lower nature get the better of us. Give the supremacy to the Holy Spirit in order to live victoriously.

The Difference between Human Knowing How to Give and God's Knowing and Giving

Notice another contrast in this verse. "If ye then, being evil, know how to give good gifts unto your children. . . ." "*Know how* to give." A natural father only *knows how* to give, but he may not necessarily give, and sometimes it is even beyond his ability to give. But God, our Heavenly Father, doesn't merely *know how* to give, He always can and will give the best, knowing what is for our eternal and infinite good. It would be a terrible thing if we had a God whom we knew to be basically evil and incapable of doing what He thought was best for us.

An earthly father may know that his child should be wiser in his decisions, display more goodness of character, and more politeness to others, but the father really can't force or give those qualities to his child. He *knows* the need, but he

151

can't *do* much about it. Well, God can! For God to *know how* to give is to give. He will give us the Spirit, not merely some mistaken manifestation of it.

The Heavenly Father gives good things to them that ask Him. The Holy Spirit is the summation of the best things in life. The Holy Spirit is the equivalent of good things as seen in Matthew 7:11. Why, therefore, should we pray for good things separately? Let us rather pray for the Holy Spirit, and we will find we have everything. May God give us the Holy Spirit, and we will have all.

Beware of Glorifying the Holy Spirit more than Christ

But don't we need the Savior? Of course we do. And the Holy Spirit, where and when He comes, takes of the things of Christ and shows them unto us. The Holy Spirit glorifies Christ, and if we find ourselves glorifying the Holy Spirit more than Christ, we are on the wrong track. The Lord said in John 16:13, 14, "He [the Holy Spirit] shall not speak of himself. . . [but] he shall glorify me." Ask for the Holy Spirit, that He may glorify Christ in you so that you may glorify Christ before others.

THINK IT OVER

1. Should Christians expect God to exempt them from the sufferings common to the rest of mankind? Why or why not? (See John 16:33.)
2. How can we know whether we are motivated by the Holy Spirit or an evil spirit? (That is, what quality or qualities does each produce in us?)
3. Whom should we glorify more — the Holy Spirit or Christ? Explain (See John 16:13, 14).

25

THE GIFT: THE HOLY SPIRIT

"If ye then, being evil, know how to give good gifts unto your children; how much more shall your Heavenly Father give the Holy Spirit to them that ask Him?" This text in Luke 11:13 mentions three things: the gift, the Giver and the receiver, and we'll take them in that order.

The gift is the Holy Spirit. The disciples, however, when they asked Him to teach them how to pray, were wondering if the Lord was going to give them a series of things that it was legitimate for them to ask for. But the Lord didn't do this. Christianity is not a legalistic religion, it is a religion of the indwelling of the Holy Spirit, who illumines our hearts to know what pleases God and to ask only for that. We think we know what is best for us, but very often we don't. Sometimes our natural self surfaces and makes requests that are not pleasing to God. But we have the assurance that God will never give in to such requests.

Jesus' First Promise of the Gift — Why Needed at This Special Time?

This verse was Christ's first promise of the gift of the Holy

Spirit to His disciples. From the first, He had made many precious promises: the Kingdom of Heaven, Divine comfort, inheritance of the earth, righteousness, mercy, a place in the Father's presence and family — all these, and many other blessings. But now, for the first time, He promises them the Holy Spirit, a promise which from this time He again and again repeats and enlarges upon, in view of His own imminent departure. This was the promise with which He sought to cheer their hearts and win them from all the worldliness and ambition they contained — the coming of the Holy Spirit.

Our Lord speaks of Him as a good gift, thus honoring and recommending the Holy Spirit to His disciples, and teaching them not only how to pray, but what to pray for. Let us then consider for a little about this good gift.

Our Lord's Experience of the Holy Spirit the Ground for Recommending Him to His Followers

We've said that Christ recommended the Holy Spirit to His disciples. But on what ground did He do this? To this question a great variety of answers might be given. But we shall content ourselves with one: Christ Himself had experience of the Spirit, and on that ground could recommend Him to His disciples. The Spirit had been a good gift to Him; therefore He could think of no better for His disciples.

Now in order that we may see what the Holy Spirit had been to the Lord Jesus, we shall look back upon Luke's narrative and we shall confine our study to this. What then has Luke, up to this point, to tell us about the Spirit in connection with our Lord's own life? Let us turn back the pages of Luke's Gospel and see.

The Holy Spirit as a Dove — Symbolizing Gentleness and Peace

"Now. . .it came to pass, that Jesus also being baptized,

and praying, the heaven was opened, and the Holy Ghost descended in a bodily shape like a dove upon him, and a voice came from heaven, which said, Thou art my beloved Son; in thee I am well pleased" (Luke 3:21, 22). The Spirit came like a dove. He comes, then, as the Spirit of gentleness and peace, for the dove is the emblem of these. And, among the many blessings He brought, gentleness and peace are certainly to be found. All the afterlife and ministry of the Master witnessed to His possession of these qualities. "Behold my servant," runs Isaiah's prophecy. "He shall not cry. . .A bruised reed shall he not break, and the smoking flax shall he not quench" (Isa. 42:1-3). The prophet spoke truly, for our Lord was the incarnation of gentleness. When John saw Him after His baptism of water and the Spirit, he said, "Behold the Lamb of God" (John 1:29), and when He marched on to His baptism of fire, "He was brought as a Lamb to the slaughter. . . yet, he opened not his mouth" (Isa. 53:7b, a). He had been baptized with the Spirit of gentleness and also of peace.

Whatever Christ had to pass through, He had inner peace. With the shadow of the cross before Him, on the threshold of His last conflict with the powers of darkness, He was at peace. In fact, He was so full of it that He could give it to others and still be rich in peace Himself. Behold Him before Pilate in the majesty of calm self-possession. Behold Him on the way to crucifixion turning to the women that followed Him and bewailed Him, saying to them, "Daughters of Jerusalem, weep not for me, but weep for yourselves, and for your children" (Luke 23:28). Behold Him on the cross, caring for His mother, saving the thief, and quietly bearing the reproaches of many. Is He not indeed the Prince of Peace? Truly, a Spirit of Peace had been given to Him.

We, Too, May Have Inner Peace in All Circumstances, through the Holy Spirit

Now surely this was the Spirit to recommend to His disciples, knowing as He did that what the Spirit was to

155

Himself He would in measure be to them. If we therefore ask for the Spirit of God, we will have peace, we will be gentle.

In the Midst of Temptation the Holy Spirit Gives Victory

Again we read, "And Jesus being full of the Holy Ghost returned from Jordan, and was led by the Spirit into the wilderness" (Luke 4:1). The Jordan River is near the city of Jericho, and it was there that our Lord was baptized, and the wilderness of the Judean Desert is not very far from it.

Observe, now, how the Holy Spirit sometimes may lead us into the wilderness for a purpose. If He leads, we are not to worry; He will also give the victory. Wasn't that the case in the life of our Lord? If He leads us into a hard place, it is so that He may make us the victors over temptation.

Notice what took place there in the wilderness. For forty days Jesus was tempted of the devil — tempted, but not overcome. He was not conquered, but He became the conqueror.

Can you imagine a life without victory? It wouldn't be worth living. Let us not mind the battles as long as we know the Lord is with us. The Lord leads us and the Lord gives us the victory.

Was not the Spirit with our Lord all through the conflict? Of course He was. When He hung on the cross, He cried, "My God, my God, why hast thou forsaken me?" (Mark 15:34). But He uttered no such cry in the wilderness, because there was no need. The Spirit brought Him into the wilderness, and when the conflict was over, angels came and ministered unto Him. But we are also told of the Spirit ministering unto Him, for it is said that He returned in the power of the Spirit to Galilee. The Holy Spirit never left Him for one single moment.

In time of need, the greatest possession we can have is not money, or a good doctor, or kind friends, but it is the presence of the Holy Spirit. Jesus returned in the power of the Spirit to

Galilee. Yet, it is not said that the Spirit, like the angels, came unto Him. No, the Spirit did not come, for since His descent upon Him the Spirit had remained with Him. The Holy Spirit never left our Lord for one single moment.

The Abiding Character of the Holy Spirit in Our Lives

It is characteristic of the Spirit to abide. "And I will pray the Father," our Lord said, "and he shall give you another Comforter, that he may abide with you for ever; even the Spirit of truth" (John 14:16, 17). What a comfort to know that the Holy Spirit abides with us in the hour of our greatest need. If we realize this, we will be victorious Christians. Of course, if we lead ourselves into temptation, we may never get out of it. But if the Holy Spirit leads us into temptation, as He did the Lord Jesus Christ, He will bring us out stronger and more victorious than when He led us in.

Naturally, we're afraid. That's why the Lord taught us to pray, "Lead us not into temptation" (Luke 11:4). We're afraid of temptation, and rightly so. But we forget that if He walks with us, temptation is nothing but an opportunity for conquest. Suffering, if He comes with us, is an opportunity for Divine joy that health could never bring to us. This is always true. When the Spirit brings us into temptation, depend upon it, it is for our good. And when He brings us in, He does not leave us there, but He brings us out strong for service or purified for the Master's presence and fellowship.

Is not this the Spirit we need today more than anything else? It is the consummation, it is the aggregate of all that is good in the hands of God — the Holy Spirit. The Spirit will not shrink from bringing us into all necessary discipline, but He will also bring us through it. He may bring us into the wilderness as He did the Savior; He may bring us through hunger and conflict; but He will bring us out strong and sanctified men and women. He may bring us into the furnace, but He will walk through its flames with us and bring us out by and by with not a hair on our heads injured, but all the better,

157

the purer, and sweeter Christians for having passed through the fires. He may put upon us many a burden and cause us to carry many a cross, but He will make our burdens wings by which to soar into the heavenly places, and each cross a rung of the ladder leading up to the throne. Let us then ask for this good gift, that we may triumph over temptation and be ready for all the perfect will of God.

The Fulfillment of Isaiah 61:1 and 2 in the Life of Our Lord

Now let's look upon one more scene in the Savior's life. Let's go, not to the wilderness, but to the synagogue at Nazareth. Here we find Jesus reading from the Book of Isaiah, as recorded in Luke 4:18 and 19: "The Spirit of the Lord is upon me, because he hath anointed me to preach the Gospel to the poor; he hath sent me to heal the brokenhearted, to preach deliverance to the captives, and recovering of sight to the blind, to set at liberty them that are bruised, to preach the acceptable year of the Lord." He sits down and says that this Scripture is fulfilled.

Now, to Him, that word "fulfilled" must have had a two-fold meaning. The prophecy was fulfilled to the people, for there He was beginning the gracious ministry of which the prophet had spoken. But the prophecy was also fulfilled in another way — it was fulfilled to Him. The prophet had represented the servant of Jehovah as having the Spirit upon Him, and there was the Lord Jesus, conscious that the prophecy was an accomplished fact in His own experience. He is anointed for His ministry of blessing among the poor, the wounded, the bound, the blind, and the oppressed, and the Spirit of the Lord is upon Him.

And so it was all through His lifetime of labor. "The Spirit of the Lord is upon me." Never at any moment was Christ bereft of that comfort, and what a comfort it must have been to Him! Men did not understand Him, but the Spirit did. Men did not love Him, but the Spirit did. Many who had followed

Him turned away from Him, but the Spirit never did. No wonder He spoke of Him as the sum of all good gifts and recommended Him to His disciples. The work which the Lord Jesus was doing they were to continue; and to do it effectively they needed the same Spirit.

Without the Holy Spirit, Our Work Is in Vain

And what of us? How glorious that we are called to the same work — the work in which the Master was engaged and the Apostles after Him — the very same work, and for it we need the very same Spirit. Without Him we shall work in vain. Yes, we may preach the Gospel to the poor, try to heal hearts that are broken, set souls at liberty that are bound and that are bruised, but unless the Spirit is upon us we will be poor preachers and poor physicians. Without the Spirit, any service is futile, is ineffective.

The Holy Spirit Alone Makes All Our Service Effective

But with the Spirit of God, all service is effective, is precious, will bring a blessing to us and those we minister to. Let us ask for and get this good gift that Jesus promised and we shall indeed be gifted — yes, gifted with power, with enthusiasm, with wisdom, with thoughtful tenderness — in short, with everything that will make our ministry for Christ a blessing to men and a thing in which angels will rejoice. May we all possess the gift that our Lord wants to give us — the Holy Spirit of God.

THINK IT OVER

1. When and under what circumstances was the Holy Spirit first promised to the disciples?
2. When did the Holy Spirit first come upon the Lord Jesus?

159

3. Where in prophecy do we find this promised with regard to the Lord Jesus?
4. Give several characteristics of the Holy Spirit beginning with the letters below:
   P _____; G _____; A _____.
   He teaches us how to P _____.
   He gives us V _____ over T _____.

26

THE GIVER AND THE RECEIVER

So much for the gift. Now the second thing we must consider is the *Giver* of the Holy Spirit — the Heavenly Father. The outstanding thing our Lord mentions about Him is the great willingness with which He gives this blessing.

Evidently some of the disciples were fathers, for Jesus says, speaking to them, "If ye then, being evil [as fathers], know how to give good gifts unto your children; how much more shall your heavenly Father give the Holy Spirit to them that ask Him?"

Our Lord knew there were parents who were kind and wise, though evil, for they not only gave gifts to their children but they had the sense to give them only good gifts. If their children asked for bread, they did not give them stones; if they asked for a fish, they did not give them a serpent; if they asked for an egg, they did not give them a scorpion.

Does God Give in the Same Measure as Earthly Parents Give?

Now, if our Lord had said only this to these men, "If ye

then, being evil, know how to give good gifts unto your children; so also will your heavenly Father give the Holy Spirit unto them that ask Him," it would have meant a great deal to them. They might have been deficient in many things, but apparently they were not deficient in paternal kindness or wisdom. Therefore, if Christ had represented the Heavenly Father to be quite as kind, quite as willing to give the Holy Spirit to them as they were to give good things to their children, they might well have rejoiced in hope of being the recipients of His goodness. And I'll venture to say that the promise would be as great to us as to them.

Parents, what would you not do for your children? A mother with her baby was once lost in a snowstorm, and to keep the child warm and alive she wrapped him in her own clothing. That mother perished, but the child lived. There are parents in this world today who would do the same for their children. Garfield's mother lived on one meal a day, that her fatherless children might have two. David would a thousand times rather have died than that Absalom should. And there are fathers that feel as tenderly toward their children as ever David did toward his.

Have you a suffering child at home? I know you would infinitely rather suffer yourself than see him suffer. Have you a child showing promise, likely to rise high in the world? I know you will sacrifice and do without, so that he may have all that is necessary for the equipment of the life at which he aims. Yes, the children must be fed, even if we go without bread. They must be clothed, though we wear patched garments.

Three Little Words that Speak of the Super-Abundance of God's Giving

The Savior, therefore, would have made a great promise if He had said that the Heavenly Father was as willing to give good things to us as we are to give good things to our children. But this is not what He said. He added the words *"how much more* shall your heavenly Father give the Holy Spirit to them that ask Him?"* That one little phrase in Luke 11:13, "how much more," tells us that our Heavenly Father not only gives as we give, but much more willingly. What a wonderful expression! "How much more." We may use it and not mean much more by it, for we consider a little thing a great deal. But from Christ's lips it covers an infinite distance. As used by Him it does mean really *much more.*

"How Much More" — an Immeasurable Distance

Look at some of the instances in which He used it, or its equivalent. "How much then is a man better than a sheep?" (Matt. 12:12). "How much more are ye better than the fowls?" (Luke 12:24). Yes, who can measure the distance between the value of a man and the value of a sheep or of a fowl? He tells us that even the sparrows, which are sold two for a farthing, are so precious to the Heavenly Father that He notes when even one of them falls to the ground, and assures us "Ye are of more value than many sparrows" — in fact He says, "the very hairs of your head are all numbered" (Luke 12:29, 30).

The distance between the value of a man and a sheep or a sparrow is immeasurable. The distance between the willingness of the Heavenly Father to give to us His Spirit and our willingness to give good things to our children is immeasurable. The Heavenly Father is infinitely willing, and, we may add, infinitely wise in the matter of giving.

When will Christians believe that the Father is infinitely willing to give the Spirit? They regard Him as having given up His Son freely, yet at the same time as possibly withholding His Spirit. But this would defeat His great purpose of mercy. The gift of the Son is powerless if the gift of the Spirit is withheld. But is God less willing to give His Spirit than He was to give His Son? What are the facts? God so loved the world that He gave us His Son. This was about nineteen centuries ago when the Heavenly Hosts proclaimed, "Glory to God in the highest, and on earth peace, good will toward men" (Luke 2:14). God gave Him up absolutely so that wicked men took Him and nailed Him to the cross. But He so gave Him only for a short time and only to a few. The Heavens from which the Son came soon received Him back again, and while He was here, there were only a few who saw His glory, who witnessed His works and listened to His words.

The Holy Spirit in the Old Testament Compared to His Coming in the New Testament

But what about the Spirit? We go back to the first days of Old Testament times and we find Him then in the world striving with men. We go back to the days of the pilgrimage to Canaan, and we find Him present there, and alas, grieved because of the hardness of the hearts of the people of God. We go back to the day of the Son's manifestation to Israel and how in the form of a dove He came down and rested upon Him. The Son has come, and He has come accompanied by the Spirit. We go back to the time when Christ the Son was received back again into His glory, and we find His followers waiting for the coming of the Spirit, in all the plenitude of His power in a fuller, grander sense than that in which He ever came before. And they did not wait in vain. The Spirit came, not as a brief sojourner, but to abide. Not to one nation, but to all flesh. Not to conduct a ministry exclusively Jewish, but to convince the world of sin and of righteousness and of judgment.

The Son Is Ours through Faith — the Spirit through Asking

No, the Father has not given the Spirit in any less degree than He gave the Son. "If ye, then, being evil, know how to give good gifts unto your children; how much more shall your Father in heaven give the Holy Spirit to them that ask Him?"

164

The Son is ours through faith. The Spirit is ours, through asking.

Who May Receive the Spirit? Any Believer, However Imperfect

And now, let us consider the receiver of the Spirit. This is important for us. Who may receive into his soul the Holy Spirit? How is He to be received? In answer to these questions, let me say that a man may be imperfect, and in some respects evil, and yet receive the Spirit.

The disciples were evil, as the Lord told us. Yet He encouraged them to ask for and so to expect the Spirit. And when the Savior refers to His disciples as being evil, He certainly has ground for it. If we read Luke's narrative even up to this point for the purpose of knowing what sort of men they were, we shall find that they had these faults: they were slow to believe; they were ambitious; they were officious; and they were revengeful.

Yet, though they were evil, they could have the Spirit. We must put away the thought that we have to wait until we are holy before we can receive the Spirit. We will never be holy *until* we receive the Spirit. He is the sanctifier and the purifier. We are to ask for Him that we may be holy, and this is how He is to be obtained, by simple asking.

We have noted some of the bad traits of the disciples. Let us now look at some of the good ones: They had left all to follow Jesus. They were most obedient. Never once do we find them saying no to any commandment of the Lord. They accepted their Master's rebukes in the spirit of meekness. They had soon learned the art of preaching the Gospel of the Kingdom. As Christ's missionaries, they did their work most satisfactorily.

Are You Satisfied with Your Prayer Life?

But there was one thing in which they felt themselves

deficient. They preached the Gospel, but they felt that they had not yet learned how to pray. This is all the more surprising when we see what an example their Master had been to them in this very matter. The first time some of them saw Him, He was praying; and as we learn simply from Luke's narrative, again and again He withdrew Himself into the wilderness and into the mountain to pray. He often continued all night in prayer. But the disciples had not learned how to pray — at any rate, satisfactorily. We may speak well *for* God, and yet very poorly *to* God. Let us pray to God to receive the Holy Spirit in His fullness. That's the greatest prayer that we can pray, for with Him we will have all things — including His help in leading us to pray as we ought, and Himself praying to the Father for us.

THINK IT OVER

1. What three words emphasize the difference in degree between His giving and the giving of earthly parents?
2. What is the blessing He gives us that earthly parents cannot bestow? (Luke 11:13).
3. Must we be "holy" before we can receive the Holy Spirit?
4. Give several contrasts between the Holy Spirit's mission in the Old Testament and in the New Testament.

I

INDEX OF SUBJECTS

Subject	*Page*
asking	78, 109, 133, 164
call, God's	
not always convenient	68
to discipleship	75, 76
common, the sacred and the	121, 124
cross, Christ's	
treasure(s) of	32
our sin and	34
Deity, Christ's	86, 111
discovery, joy of	27
evil, symbols of	123
excuses	37
excuses, selfish	68
faith, seeking in	32
faithfulness, God's	13
fatherhood, God's: preface	37, 121, 130
friend, the importunate	11
generosity, God's	38, 41, 139
giving (God's, our)	39, 161, 162
God: our utter dependence on him	17
a hidden treasure	34
a treasure hunter	34
our relation to Him	118
never mocks us	129
never deceives us	137, 147
perfection of	140

grace, throne of 20
   treasures of 28
hider, God the 27
Holy Spirit, infilling of the 150
   Christ and the 152
   gift of the 153, 165
   peace through the 155
   abiding of the 157
   and service 159
   Old Testament, New Testament 164
humanity, Christ's 124
inconvenience, fear of 67
invitation, God's 101
knocking, God's and our 109
knowing/giving: divine and human 151
knowledge, God's 142
loaves, three 21, 22
mercies, God's common 102
name — Jesus, the 43
needs, spiritual 18
   as God sees them 44
   of others 46
parable, a missionary 49
peace, God's 135, 155
prayer(s)
   persistence in 11, 105
   getting answers to 37, 138
   God does not answer 43, 138
   delays in answer to 49
   intercessory 51
   right motive(s) in 51, 142
   reasonableness, insistency and
      urgency in 55
   for which we are to take no denial 56
   why God demands importunity in 58
   as begging for others 60

as altruism	63
for as much as we need	78
how God answers	82
laws of nature, miracles and	
answers to	82
predestination and	85, 91
answers to contradictory	87
privilege of	89
limitations of what we may ask in	90
In Jesus' Name	90
Christ our great example in	93
Jesus our intermediary in	93
Jesus our example in	94
a value in itself	96, 101
and proper limitations on our requests	97
and thought	98
a common need of all	102
and special graces	103
God takes the initiative in	104
arrogance vs. humility in	104
as begging	110
and submission	113
God will answer	118, 133
and the Holy Spirit	122
character of	125
for necessities, not luxuries	126, 143
unexpected answers to	131
God's help in	134
life of	165
preaching, practicing and	73
preachers	18
promises, God's	40
empty	46
of answered prayer	57
dependability of God's	81
how we know we can trust	82

to his seekers 117
question
    one, 13 — answers to 14
    two, 13 — answers to 17
regeneration 102
response, God's response to our 106
revelation, God's highest 32
salvation for the lost 22, 102, 115, 143
searching, discipline of 33
seeker, man the 27, 115, 116
    God the 115
seeking, finding and 26, 27, 115, 116, 117
service, self realization found in 77
sorrow, comfort in 21
spirits, evil 149
suffering 45, 148
temptation, grace in 22
    victory in 156
treasure hunt, invitation to a 25
    why a 33
treasure(s), of darkness 28
    in the shadow of death 29
    in unlikely places 31
    God's richest 32
    unlikeliest place of all to find 32
values, God's and our 131
Virgin Mary, the 102
will, sovereignty of God's 85
    of man and prayer 85
Word, God's 57

(For fuller index see Index of Greek Words)

II

INDEX OF ENGLISH WORDS

English	Greek	Scripture	Page
and	*kai*	Luke 11:8, 9	81, 116
ask	*aite-oo*	Luke 11:9, 13	
		John 16:23	106, 110-1
			142
(on an equal basis)	*eroota-oo*	John 14:16	
		16:23, 26	
		17:8, 16, 20	110, 111
bad	*kakos*		140, 141
	phaulos		140
be (basically or intrinsically)	*huparchoo*	Luke 11:13	151
bread	*artos*	Luke 11:11	124
beggar	*epaitees*		110
blow (of wind)	*pne-oo*		149
faithful	*pistos*	I Cor. 1:9	82
fill	*pleero-oo*	Eph. 5:18	150
find	*heuriskoo*	Luke 11:9	116
gift	*doma*	Matt. 7:11	140
give	*didoomi*	Luke 11:9	113
God	*Theos*	I Cor. 1:9	82
good	*agathos*	Matt. 7:11	
		Luke 11:13	140, 141
I	*egoo*	Luke 11:8, 9	81
impoliteness	*anaideia*	Luke 11:8	59, 77
knock	*krou-oo*	Luke 11:9	106
know how	*oida*	Luke 11:13	142

love	*agapee*	I John 4:18	63
perfect	*teleios, a, on*	I John 4:18	63
say	*legoo*	Luke 11:8, 9	81, 89
seek	*zeete-oo*	Luke 11:9	106, 115-6
sense, good	*soophrosunee*	Acts 26:25	97
speak	*lale-oo*		89
spirit	*pneuma*	Luke 11:13	149
the	*ho*	Romans 12:3	
		I Cor. 1:9	82, 98
think	*phrone-oo*	Romans 12:3	98
think sensibly	*soophrone-oo*	Romans 12:3	98
unto	*eis*	Romans 12:3	98
wicked (actively)	*poneeros*	Luke 11:13	140-1
Word	Logos		89

III

INDEX OF GREEK WORDS

Greek	English	Scripture	Page
agapee	love	I John 4:18	63
agatha,			
agathos	good	Matt. 7:11	
	beneficial	Luke 11:13	140, 141
aite-oo,			
aiteeseete,	ask	Luke 11:9, 13	106, 110
aiteite,		John 16:23	111, 142
anaideia,	impoliteness,		
anaideis	insolence	Luke 11:8	59, 77
arton, artos	bread	Luke 11:11	124
didoomi,			
dotheesetai	give	Luke 11:9	113
doma, domata	gift	Matt. 7:11	140
egoo	I	Luke 11:8, 9	81
eis	to, unto	Romans 12:3	98
epaitees	beggar		110
eroota-oo,	ask (on an	John 16:23, 26	
erooteesete	equal basis)	14:16; 17:9,	
		16, 20	110, 111
heuriskoo,			
heureesete	find	Luke 11:9	116
huparchoo,	be (basically) or		
huparchontes	(intrinsically)	Luke 11:13	151
ho	the	Romans 12:3	
		I Cor. 1:9	82, 98
		Luke 11:9	

kagoo,
  see *kai* and
  egoo

kai	and	Luke 11:8, 9	81, 116
kakos	bad		140, 141
krou-oo,			
krouete	knock	Luke 11:9	106
lale-oo	speak		89
legoo	say, tell	Luke 11:8, 9	81, 89
Logos	Word		89
oida,	know,		
oidate	(instinctively)		
	know how	Luke 11:13	142
phaulos	bad		140
phrone-oo,			
phronein	think	Romans 12:3	98
pistos	faithful	I Cor. 1:9	82
pleero-oo,			
pleerootheete,	fill		
pleerousthe	fulfill	Eph. 5:18	150
pne-oo	blow (of wind)		149
pneuma	spirit, wind	Luke 11:13	149
poneeros,	wicked		
poneeroi	(actively)	Luke 11:13	140, 141
soophrone-oo,			
soophronein	think sensibly	Romans 12:3	98
soophrosunee	sense, good,		
	sobriety	Acts 25, 26	97
teleios, a, on	complete,		
	perfect	I John 4:18	63
Theos	God	I Cor. 1:9	82
to,			
see *ho*			
zeeteite,			
zeete-oo	seek	Luke 11:9	106, 115-6

IV

INDEX OF SCRIPTURE VERSES

Scripture Verse   *Page*

Scripture Verse	Page
Psalms 23:4	30
Proverbs 25:2	33
Isaiah 45:3	28
Isaiah 61:1, 2	158
Matthew 7:11	150, 152
Luke 1:46	102
Luke 4:1	156
Luke 4:18, 19	158
Luke 11:4	157
Luke 11:9	102, 103, 109, 110
John 16:13, 14	152
John 14:16, 17	157
Acts 17:24, 27	34
Romans 8:26	134
II Corinthians 12:9	137
Ephesians 5:18, 19, 20	150
Colossians 1:17	86
Colossians 2:9	86
Hebrews 5:7, 8	45
Hebrews 6:4-6	144

V

ILLUSTRATION INDEX

Subject			Page
accomplishment			26
death, shadow of			29
doubts, conquest of			96
prayer and			96
friend, importunate			11
giving		39,	74
God not a vending machine			17
leprosy			70
lives, giving our	70,	71,	74
mediator, Christ the			93
parents, sacrifice of			162
parish, a difficult			70
practice, preaching and			73
prayer, boldness in			104
Christ's presence in		112,	113
literal answers to			133
unanswered			138
prayers, contradictory and various			87
temptation, prayer and			28
treasures in unlikely places		31,	32
visitation, pastoral			47
will, God's knowledge and			94

Other Books by Dr. Spiros Zodhiates

Studies on I Corinthians

1. A Richer Life for You in Christ   pg. 487
   I Corinthians Chapter 1
   clothbound and vinyl
2. A Revolutionary Mystery   Paper pg. 278
   I Corinthians Chapter 2
3. Getting the Most Out of Life   Paper pg. 380
   I Corinthians Chapter 3
4. You and Public Opinion   Paper pg. 196
   I Corinthians Chapter 4:1-5
5. Formula For Happiness   Paper pg. 270
   I Corinthians Chapter 4:6-21
6. The Gifts of the Holy Spirit   Paper pg. 491
   and The Holy Spirit's Baptism and Infilling
   I Corinthians 12:1-13
7. The Holy Spirit's Baptism and Infilling   Paper pg. 55
   I Corinthians 12:13 and related passages
8. Variety in Christ's Body and the Better   Paper pg. 259
   Gifts of the Holy Spirit
   I Corinthians 12:14-31
9. I Corinthians 12 Two Volume Set
10. To Love is to Live   Hardback pg. 365
11. Tongues!?   Paper pg. 192
    I Corinthians 14:1-33
12. Conquering the Fear of Death   Paper pg. 869
    I Corinthians 15

Studies on Matthew

1. The Pursuit of Happiness   Paper pg. 695
   The Beatitudes Matthew 5:1-12
            Luke 6:20-26

2. A Christian View of War and Peace   Paper pg. 128
   Matthew 5:9 and related passages on peacemaking

3. The Lord's Prayer   Paper pg. 411
   Matthew 6:9-13; Luke 11:1-4

Studies on Luke

1. The Song of the Virgin   Paper pg. 145
   Luke 1:28, 46-55
2. Why Pray? The Parable of the Persistent Friend   Paper pg. 176
3. The Demon World and Jesus: The Parable   Paper pg. 184
   of the Demon departing, wandering in dry places
   and later returning as if it were to an empty
   house bringing along seven other spirits.
   Luke 11:14-32
4. Conscience: The Parable of the Lamp and the   Paper pg. 140
   Light in man becoming darkness
   Luke 11:33-36
5. Why God Permits Accidents   Paper pg. 87
   Luke 13:1-9
6. Did Jesus Teach Capitalism?   Paper pg. 102
   The Parable of the Pounds
   Luke 19:11-27
7. How to Manage Money: The Parable of   Paper pg. 245
   the Steward of Unrighteousness (money)
   Luke 16:1-13

Studies in John's Gospel

1. Was Christ God?   Paper pg. 362
   John 1:1-18 and related passages

Studies on James

1. The Work of Faith   Paper pg. 223
   James 1:1-2:13
2. The Labor of Love   Paper pg. 376
   James 2:14-4:12
3. The Patience of Hope   Paper pg. 299
   James 14:13-5:20

Three-Volume Set in handsome slip cover

Miscellaneous Titles

1. Christianity Not Just a Religion   Paper pg. 166
2. Life After Death   Paper pg. 256
3. Resurrection: True or False?   Paper pg. 130
4. The Perfect Gift   Paper pg. 99
5. You Can Be a Winner   Paper pg. 216
6. Who is Worth Following?   Paper pg. 153
   The First Two Commandments of Christ: Repent and
   Follow After Me